MW01505994

PRAISE FOR
GAIN BIG AND GIVE BACK

"*Personal finance is more personal than it is finance, so I was thrilled to see that author Patrick Rush acknowledges this from the very beginning in* Gain Big and Give Back. *His insight is couched in meaningful doses of vulnerability, inviting us into his story as he shares his hard-earned wisdom. It is at this intersection of life and money where the book excels, calling us to examine our personal values even before it extols evidence-based financial planning strategies that should also improve our bottom lines.*"

—TIM MAURER
CFP®, director of advisor development, speaker, author

"*Managing your wealth and retirement goals requires intimate and personal knowledge. Patrick completes that circle of trust as he shares intimate and personal knowledge about himself in* Gain Big and Give Back. *What does it take to write a book like this? I imagine that it starts with a passion for the topic, deeply researched and blended with practical experience for a robust working knowledge. Throw in strong communication skills and the veracity to practice what you preach. That's what it takes to help investors like me to navigate and filter the consequences of investment options and complex financial issues. That's what I get as a TFA client. And now Patrick has authored* Gain Big and Give Back, *which summarizes it all.*"

—PAUL MEGLIOLA
President, Megliola Management Services, Inc.

"Following my fourteen-year career as President of University of the Pacific, I determined I needed to find a financial advisor. I decided to interview individuals in much the same way that I had interviewed fund managers and endowment advisors at the university. My wife and I met with seven Certified Financial Planners. It was an eye-opening experience, as there was great variability among the group. It wasn't until we met with Patrick Rush at Triad Financial Advisors that we felt we had met a person who would put our financial interests first. Time and time again over the past six years, my confidence in our partnering with Patrick has only grown. One recent example of this was his ability to demonstrate how we could make generous gifts during our lifetime, 'with warm hands instead of cold ones.' The decision better reflected our values and priorities and permitted us to enjoy seeing the immediate impact of those gifts. In his book Gain Big and Give Back: Financial Planning with Intention, *Patrick Rush describes his approach to financial planning. It will help you secure a financial advisor who will put you and your family's interests first in achieving your financial and personal goals."*

—DR. DONALD V. DEROSA

President emeritus, University of the Pacific

"Patrick Rush is a successful business owner, yet that's just the tip of the iceberg. He's a committed husband and father, a loyal friend, and someone that serves his community in countless ways. This book is just one of many examples of Patrick's passion for positively impacting those around him. A true servant-leader!"

—WES MILLER

Men's head basketball coach, University of North Carolina at Greensboro

"Rush's great skill lies in his ability to articulate a financial strategy guided by values. Focus on what is important. Define the kind of life you want to live and how you want to give back. Financial goals and investment strategies follow. Clients working with Patrick Rush and his colleagues at Triad Financial Advisors are fortunate indeed."

—DR. LINDA BRADY

Chancellor emerita, University of North Carolina at Greensboro

GAIN BIG

AND

GIVE BACK

PATRICK RUSH

GAIN BIG

FINANCIAL
PLANNING
WITH INTENTION

AND
GIVE BACK

ForbesBooks

Published by ForbesBooks, Charleston, South Carolina.
Member of Advantage Media Group.

ForbesBooks is a registered trademark, and the ForbesBooks colophon is a trademark of Forbes Media, LLC.

Printed in the United States of America.

10 9 8 7 6 5 4 3 2 1

ISBN: 978-1-95086-311-2
LCCN: 2020911678

Cover design by David Taylor.
Layout design by Mary Hamilton.

This custom publication is intended to provide accurate information and the opinions of the author in regard to the subject matter covered. It is sold with the understanding that the publisher, Advantage|ForbesBooks, is not engaged in rendering legal, financial, or professional services of any kind. If legal advice or other expert assistance is required, the reader is advised to seek the services of a competent professional.

Advantage Media Group is proud to be a part of the Tree Neutral® program. Tree Neutral offsets the number of trees consumed in the production and printing of this book by taking proactive steps such as planting trees in direct proportion to the number of trees used to print books. To learn more about Tree Neutral, please visit **www.treeneutral.com**.

Since 1917, Forbes has remained steadfast in its mission to serve as the defining voice of entrepreneurial capitalism. ForbesBooks, launched in 2016 through a partnership with Advantage Media Group, furthers that aim by helping business and thought leaders bring their stories, passion, and knowledge to the forefront in custom books. Opinions expressed by ForbesBooks authors are their own. To be considered for publication, please visit **www.forbesbooks.com**.

*To Mom and Pop: Thank you for always believing in me
and demonstrating that hard work and integrity are not optional.*

CONTENTS

INTRODUCTION

The rich don't just *have* a lot of money. They also know how to make it, spend it, save it, and share it in a way that turns money into wealth.

This know-how does not come from elite expertise or secret wisdom. It's not accessible to only the cleverest people, to Wall Street scions or mathematical geniuses who have figured out how to game the market. On the contrary, the methods for building wealth are *simple* and can be mastered by anyone.

So many people—including high earners—stumble through life making the same mistakes that chip away at their portfolios (and, ultimately, their lifestyles). I myself had to learn the techniques of money management on my own. My parents, like many Americans, worked hard but understood little about saving and investment. My dad was a teamster who worked various jobs in the Chicago trucking industry, from foreman to forklift operator, and my mom, whose educational background was in special education, was a hospital administrator as well as an alderwoman in my hometown of Palos Hills, Illinois. They were diligent, dedicated, college-educated folk, and thanks to their strong work ethic and rock-solid values, my siblings and I enjoyed a comfortable middle-class life for the most part. We lacked luxuries, but we never went without. We had what we needed. We were happy. And to us kids, everything seemed okay.

And yet, my parents did struggle at times. They saved little. Investment was an unfamiliar concept. They lacked a strong financial plan. A few unforeseeable misfortunes knocked them off track, and things got so bad that my parents went into bankruptcy. Our phone rang day and night from creditors badgering my father to pay his bills. During this period, my parents still made sure we had clothes on our backs and food on the table—they sheltered us from the physical and psychological brunt of bankruptcy—but I'll never forget sitting in the next room listening to my dad plead with the bill collectors to give him time, to trust him that next month, he'd come up with the payment.

Even as a child, I could sense the helplessness and hopelessness in his voice—that feeling of letting his family down, even though he was doing everything in his power to keep us healthy, happy, and well fed.

Growing up, you don't realize how much your parents sacrifice for you. As a bright kid who showed early academic promise, my parents wanted me to get the kind of education that our Chicago-land public schools couldn't provide, so I studied at a Montessori school—oblivious, as kids so often are, of the vast expense of such an opportunity. And that educational leg up allowed me to skip a grade and get on the fast track to the path that later led to success as an adult.

Years later, when I was around thirty, I was sitting across from my dad in a brightly lit diner, half-eaten plates of bacon and eggs and mugs of strong coffee between us. He was a little older but still had the same youthful spark and stoic strength in his eye. "Dad," I asked, "how could you ever afford to send me to a private Montessori school? It must have cost a fortune."

He smiled. "It did. But I worked out a deal."

"A deal?" I thought of how the teamsters in Chicago were notoriously mobbed up during that era and for a second wondered about the unlikely notion that my old man had called in a favor to strong-arm the friendly administrators of the Montessori school.

"I made an arrangement with the school: they'd let you study for a reduced rate, and I'd work as a janitor on the night shift. That was how we were able to send you there," he said.

I teared up. In fact, I was so moved that I had to get up from the table for a second and collect myself. I don't think he saw his effort as heroic—he just did what had to be done so his son could get a boost in a competitive and sometimes unforgiving world. "Man," I thought, "I owe this guy and my mom the world."

This conversation was still in the back of my mind a few months later, when I was shopping at Target one chilly November afternoon. A petite young woman with dark hair, olive skin, and Cuban features caught my eye. She was standing by the Icee machine, dispensing its sugary, frozen slush into a plastic cup. I've been a devotee of Icees (also known as Slurpees) since I was a kid, in any kind of weather.

"I guess you're as weird as I am," I joked. "Eating Icees when it's thirty-five degrees out."

She laughed and admitted that the cold didn't repress her Icee predilection either. We got to chatting. Instantly, I was enamored by her big brown eyes and her radiant demeanor. I teased her about her choice of flavor (a mix of blueberry and cherry). I myself opted for the Coke flavor. And I knew I had to get her phone number.

Fifteen years later, we're still together. I still think Christina's Icee flavor preferences are all wrong. But I love everything else about her.

In 2008, Christina and I got married and started a family, a tumultuous process of emotional highs and lows as we struggled for a long time to have kids. We went through the whole wrenching process of fertility treatments, the heartbreak of multiple miscarriages.

Finally, after so much disappointment and hope and trying and waiting, she gave birth to a beautiful baby girl we named Havana. But our daughter was born at twenty-six weeks—fourteen weeks premature. A fragile little girl, fighting for her life in the neonatal ICU, her one-and-a-half-pound body crisscrossed with plastic tubes and surrounded by beeping monitors.

I was beginning to understand what my dad had been through: the boundless willpower that comes from parental love brushing up against the maddening sense of helplessness when faced with things over which we have no control, despite our burning desire to make everything right.

And yet, Havana pulled through. It was a long ordeal, but it made us all stronger as a family. A few years later, we added twin boys to the mix. The experience of having kids gave me new perspective and made me think hard about my own life and role as a new father. I was eager to protect my family from any kind of hardship. I couldn't control everything, but I could at least provide the kind of financial cushion that would ensure they would always be free of want, free of need, free of worry.

The birth of my daughter coincided with another major life change. Around that time, I had just left Merrill Lynch to start my own business and was working hard to provide the best possible service for my first clients. But they were more interested in how Christina and Havana were doing.

I was deeply moved by their empathy and inspired by the fact that they cared about me as a person, not just as the guy managing their money. And I knew I cared about them too. I vowed to always do the right thing for them. To help them build the life they dreamed of, and to do it ethically and with the client first in mind.

Being a financial advisor and an entrepreneur, I saw, wasn't just about expanding the bottom line or maximizing returns. It was about people. It was about providing the best possible life for my clients, my family, and everyone I cared about.

This book will empower you to do the same, for you and yours.

In *Gain Big and Give Back*, I will teach you that financial confidence is the result of applying basic know-how to your hard-earned dollars. The book is targeted primarily to baby boomers and retirees with a high net worth, but the lessons are applicable for anyone of any age and at any stage in their financial journey.

> Being a financial advisor and an entrepreneur, I saw, wasn't just about expanding the bottom line or maximizing returns. It was about people.

In my work as a financial advisor and planner, I've seen people grow great fortunes just by following a remarkably simple system, saving and investing wisely, and planning ahead. I've also seen the opposite happen: people destroy their nest egg through bad decisions, lack of a plan, and other totally avoidable pitfalls. I've seen people with a seemingly inexhaustible portfolio squander it bit by bit until faced with the miserable prospect of a destitute retirement.

I've spent the past twenty-plus years working at every level of the financial industry, from clerk at the Chicago Mercantile Exchange to sole owner and CEO of Greensboro, North Carolina–based Triad Financial Advisors, a twenty-employee investment advisory firm recognized by the *Financial Times*, *Barron's*, and *Forbes* as one of the top financial advising firms in the US. Throughout my career, I have helped thousands of investors learn how to live a life of wealth and abundance.

Some financial writers are just teachers focused on the theory, while others are advisors focused on the practice. I have experience doing both, as for much of my professional life, I've taught classes to those looking to brush up on their financial literacy and develop confidence in managing money.

> ## The problem for investors today is not lack of information. The problem is an overabundance of information.

The problem for investors today is not lack of information. The problem is an *overabundance* of information, so much that it can make your head spin. Where do you turn for guidance? Who will help you separate the wheat from the chaff?

It's not enough to simply "hire an advisor," because you just run into the same problem: there are countless advisors, but which one is the best one for you? Picking the wrong one can lead you down the wrong path, as unfortunately, some advisors are working more for their own benefit than that of their clients.

The key is educating yourself in the simple secrets behind the following:

- Understanding the shortcomings of the financial advice industry (chapter 2)

- Creating a financial plan that works for you and your family (chapter 3)

- Leveraging the power of evidence-based investing (chapter 4)

- Earning a portfolio paycheck that'll provide you income for the entirety of your retirement (chapter 5)

- Taking advantage of tax efficiencies that work for retirees (chapter 6)

- Determining your best options for healthcare (chapter 7)

- Making charitable giving an important and efficient part of your retirement planning (chapter 8)

- Having frank discussions with your family about financial matters (chapter 9)

- Understanding how hiring an advisor can benefit you and how to choose the right one (chapter 10)

In my life, I've always sought to learn from millionaires and then share the knowledge with everyone else. If you want to retire with confidence, then you can start by reading this book, where you will learn the fundamentals of both *gaining big* and *giving back*.

After all, many wealthy investors don't just want to hoard their gains. They also want to have conversations about charity, civic duty, and moral responsibility—financial planning guided by values, not just valuables.

CHAPTER ONE

IS MANAGING YOUR MONEY REALLY THAT COMPLICATED?

L et me tell you about the time I got fired.

Not from a job, but fired by a client. I had started working with Denise in 2005. She was making over two million dollars per year as a top mortgage executive, in a booming housing industry where people seemed to refinance their homes every year.

Being in the right place in the right industry at the right time had made her successful, but she was also extremely hardworking, charismatic, and good with money. She was saving a lot into her 401(k), brokerage account, and a nonqualified deferred compensation plan. The nonqualified deferred compensation plan assets were 100 percent invested in her employer stock, but the company was strong, and housing, as everyone knows (or thought they knew) is the invincible backbone of the American economy. Even in the event of a downturn, she thought she'd be fine.

She also purchased an amazing beach property for $1.4 million and was generally living a fast-paced life, jet-setting around the country and hobnobbing with the who's who of Greensboro.

I cautioned her about putting too many eggs in one basket— that is, her company stock. We always tell clients not to invest more than 5 to 10 percent of their portfolio in one company, especially if that company is responsible for providing your income and benefits. It's dangerous to stake so much on one firm—no company, no matter how big, is invincible. I also counseled her that the beach home was not the savviest of investments. A vacation property or second home provides fun and joy but rarely works out financially.

Then the subprime mortgage bubble popped in 2007, followed by a full-blown global financial meltdown in 2008. She was fired, but it probably didn't matter much because her employer—the vaunted mortgage company that had made her rich—also bit the dust. (It would later be acquired for a fraction of what it was once worth.) Not only had she lost her job, but the shares of stock in her deferred compensation plan cratered, like most mortgage and bank stocks. And her new beach house was suddenly worth half its initial value.

Then, she fired me.

It was a humbling, gut-wrenching experience that made me feel horrible for a long time. To make matters worse, she replaced me with a broker who convinced her to dump her $1 million rollover IRA and $2 million brokerage account into annuities, assuring her that she would never lose money again because the annuities had guarantees. But he didn't explain to her the many drawbacks of annuities. He took advantage of her crushed ego and sense of desperation to talk her into tying up a huge amount of capital in a less-than-favorable investment.

A couple of years went by, and she called me to tell me that she wanted to work with me again. She was back on her feet, and the financial markets were making a strong comeback. Still hurt that she had ever fired me in the first place, I invited her to my office for a meeting. I was stunned to find out all of her assets were now invested in annuities with seven-year surrender penalties and 3.5 percent internal fees. The broker had made over $200,000 in commissions selling her the annuities—no wonder he was so sweet on them. She was "safe" in annuities, but her returns were dismal compared to the performance of the stock market. But their stiff surrender penalties made it unviable to liquidate them.

Regardless, I took her back as a client, and we built a new financial plan from scratch. We focused on the future instead of the past, concentrating on building a diversified portfolio that she could tolerate in both good and bad markets and saving as much money as she could from her paycheck at her new job. We also touched on other critical aspects of planning that her former advisor never addressed, such as long-term care insurance, estate planning, and renting out the beach home that was still greatly underwater in value.

Ultimately, we made it work, and I'm happy to say she's doing well now and remains a loyal client. But it didn't have to be this complicated!

Keeping it simple—following a set of simple, proven steps to building wealth while preventing costly and avoidable errors—is the difference between spending your retirement having the life you've dreamed and merely dreaming about the life you could have had.

> Keeping it simple—following a set of simple, proven steps to building wealth while preventing costly and avoidable errors— is the difference between spending your retirement having the life you've dreamed and merely dreaming about the life you could have had.

WHY IS MOST INVESTING SO COMPLICATED?

It's all too common to chase investment "opportunities" while ignoring financial fundamentals that in the long run would make you a millionaire. Investing doesn't have to be complicated; in fact, it shouldn't be. The more complicated it is, the more likely someone is making more money from your investment than you are.

Too many people, especially as they start moving up in income, are enticed by financial pop and flash. They hear at a cocktail party or from their buddy on the golf course about some great real estate investment or some private equity venture (very high risk) or some up-and-coming tech stock. Or they're seduced by intricate-sounding names of financial instruments that seem to grow ever more complex: structured notes, variable and indexed annuities, alternative investments, collateralized debt obligations. Yet more often than not, these things don't lead anywhere, or their high fees will eat away at your profit.

Follow the KISS approach: keep it simple, stupid. That means buy-and-hold investment in unflashy yet proven equities with low fees and an absence of bells and whistles. Avoid products that are expensive (e.g., annuities, which are often saddled with high and/or hidden fees) or highly speculative (e.g., hedge funds, high-risk stocks). Pursue mostly passive, value investing while minimizing trading, and don't attempt to time the market, which is something a vanishingly small number of people can do consistently over the long term.

Warren Buffett has popularized this kind of strategy, and the results speak for themselves: a famously unflashy self-made mogul with a net worth of around $87 billion, Buffett is one of the world's richest men. And he built his empire by following the same simple, value-driven strategy of holding on to quality assets over a long timeline.

There's a mountain of evidence backing the superiority of passive, buy-and-hold investment for long-term wealth generation. For one, capital markets tend to rise over time. Although periods of volatility and intermittent market crashes can decimate a portfolio, nearly one hundred years of historical data tell us that markets always eventually recover from downturns. The law of averages works in your favor if you simply buy proven investments and hold them for decades.

Consider these facts: in 2019, two-thirds of large-cap funds underperformed the S&P 500, according to S&P Dow Jones Indices' SPIVA US Scorecard, which measures the performance of various actively traded fund categories (small-cap, large-cap, domestic, international, etc.) against a corresponding benchmark index fund. Most actively managed large-cap equity funds (71 percent) underperformed the S&P 500 for the tenth consecutive one-year period.

In fact, 89 percent of large-cap equity funds underperformed the S&P 500 over the past decade, and it didn't matter what the Federal Reserve was doing—the Fed was on hold from 2010 to 2015, it raised interest rates from 2015 to 2018, and it cut interest rates in 2019.

Even more striking, over a fifteen-year period, around 90 percent of small-cap, mid-cap, and large-cap fund managers under-performed their respective benchmarks.[1] And these are some of the smartest people on Wall Street.

High-flying hedge funds—many of them run and staffed by financial wizards and mathematical geniuses—also struggle to beat the returns of a simple index fund that tracks the S&P 500 or Dow Jones Industrial Average. For example, from January 2009 to December 2018, hedge funds averaged a return of around 6 percent; meanwhile, the S&P 500 leaped by 15 percent annually.[2] In 2019, a fantastic year for the market, hedge funds earned investors a comparatively measly 7 percent, trailing the market as a whole.[3] If hedge funds can't justify their high fees and can't even beat a simple index fund, why bother with them?

---

1   Berlinda Liu and Philip Brzenk, SPIVA® US Scorecard: Mid-Year 2019, S&P Dow Jones Industries, 2019, https://www.spindices.com/documents/spiva/spiva-us-mid-year-2019.pdf. The same report tells us that bond funds were really no different: "Government bond funds in general had a miserable decade, as an incredible 99% of long bond funds failed to clear the bar over the past 10 years, along with 80% and 70% of intermediate and short-end bond funds, respectively."

2   Michelle Celarier, "What the Hell Happened to Hedge Funds?" *Worth*, January 2, 2019, https://www.worth.com/what-the-hell-happened-to-hedge-funds/.

3   Andrea Riquier, "Hedge-Fund Returns Badly Lagged the Stock Market in 2019," *MarketWatch*, January 2, 2020, https://www.marketwatch.com/story/hedge-fund-returns-badly-lagged-behind-the-stock-market-in-2019-2020-01-02.

It's just very hard to beat the market over time. Fortunately, you don't have to try. While there are thousands of complicated ways to invest your money, there are only a handful of proven ways to grow wealth. Keep it simple, stupid! Sit back, relax, and let the markets do what they've done consistently for decades: make money from your money, without your active involvement.

This is what I tell the classes I teach at universities and community colleges to preretirees and postretirees. This is the basis of my professional practice for over twenty years and the paradigm that has helped Triad Financial Advisors (TFA) rocket from a little-known upstart firm to a nationally recognized little-engine-that-could powerhouse in just a few short years.

> While there are thousands of complicated ways to invest your money, there are only a handful of proven ways to grow wealth. Keep it simple, stupid!

THE BIG SIX

The wealthiest Americans have grown their fortunes by understanding financial basics and following a set of fundamentals—what I describe as *the big six approaches to wealth management*, which this book will expound on:

1. A FINANCIAL PLAN—YOUR MOST IMPORTANT WEALTH AND CONFIDENCE-BUILDING TOOL

This is number one for a reason: we make sure everybody has a financial plan in place before we start making investment recommendations. That plan addresses budgeting and expenses, investing, insurance, long-term care, estate planning, tax planning, benefits, and other matters critical to your long-term financial success. It also establishes a clear list of specific financial goals, which is the starting point for any lifetime wealth-building strategy.

2. EVIDENCE-BASED INVESTING

Evidence-based investment maximizes returns by pursuing a proven investment strategy backed by facts, reason, and historical data.

At TFA, Dimensional Fund Advisors makes up a big part of our approach to evidence-based investment. They're one of the largest mutual fund companies in the world, but they're not accessible to retail investors. You can purchase their funds only through a select group of advisors. But it's a low-cost approach with solid returns that gives you the most bang for your buck.

3. A PORTFOLIO PAYCHECK: HOW YOU MAKE INCOME IN RETIREMENT

One of the biggest sources of anxiety for retirees is how they're going to live comfortably and manage expenses when they don't have a paycheck coming in. Here, we find the right way to let you draw a "paycheck" from your portfolio without taking unnecessary risks that could jeopardize your lifelong savings.

4. TAXES, AND HOW EFFICIENCIES CAN BENEFIT YOU

Tax law is confusing in the best of times; since the passage of the 2018 tax law and subsequent passage of the SECURE Act of 2019, more people than ever are uncertain about how the law applies to them and how to optimize their tax situation. I'll teach you how to find hidden opportunities and avoid costly mistakes to be more tax efficient.

5. CHOOSING THE RIGHT HEALTHCARE

To live a healthy, happy life, you'll need proper medical care at your disposal, but the fear of losing employer-provided health insurance is often a barrier to people who want to retire early. After retirement, the healthcare field can feel like an expensive, perplexing labyrinth of choices. Moreover, not being properly covered (or buying coverage with sky-high premiums) can wreck your savings.

I'll advise you on how to navigate this challenging part of financial planning and tell you how you can qualify for health insurance subsidies and other benefits, even if you're a millionaire.

6. CHARITABLE GIVING

Community involvement is a big part of our philosophy at TFA and a powerful motivator for me personally. It's a frequently neglected area of financial planning, but it's important for one's financial health *and* spiritual and emotional well-being. For those who are passionate about charitable giving, I'll explain how to do it in a financially prudent, tax-efficient manner.

The means of building and maintaining vast wealth are not a secret. It's available to everyone. It's an approach I use in managing money for my own clients, many of whom have a net worth in the seven or eight figures. Learn this approach so that you can put your trust in advisors who do the same.

TAKEAWAYS:

1. Financial planning and investing are mutually dependent. Sound investment strategy depends on a thorough financial plan, and no plan is complete without addressing investment.

2. So-called experts can't beat the market, so why do you think you can? Avoid active trading of higher-risk, higher-cost investment products and stick to the basics: value investing in stalwart, low-fee funds that will make you rich over the long term.

3. Slow and steady wins the race. And all that glitters is not gold. Clichés? Yes, definitely. But all clichés possess a kernel of truth, and these lessons apply to wealth building too. Just ask Warren Buffett. He eschews flash for frugality and has lived in the same modest house for fifty years, but he's amassed $87 billion in a half century of prudent investing.

CHAPTER TWO

ALL THAT GLITTERS IS NOT GOLD

The Dirty Secrets of the Financial Services Industry

Building wealth is a lifelong project that should be undertaken with the counsel of an advisor. Proceeding without one is perilous. And working with a bad advisor might be even worse. Unfortunately, there are many poor advisors out there who work for themselves first and their clients second.

Terrence and Barbara have been clients of mine for seven years. He's a psychiatrist with a sharp mind and has excellent listening skills (comes with the territory). She's a retired school administrator with a good heart and an infectious energy.

We first met when they attended one of my seminars at a community college; after the seminar, they signed up as clients. Before that, they had been working with both an advisor *and* a CPA, but the seminar made them realize they needed some additional professional guidance to sort out their messy financial picture.

We sat down together, and I took a look under the hood. What I saw there was a case study in the danger of getting advice from the wrong people.

- As a self-employed psychiatrist, Terrence was making only $6,000 in annual traditional IRA contributions instead of using a SEP-IRA plan that would allow him to contribute over $50,000 a year. His income was over $220,000, and a SEP-IRA is a much better vehicle than a traditional IRA since he didn't have access to a group 401(k) plan and was willing and able to contribute much more to savings. In addition, he could make $6,000 a year (today it's $7,000 per year) *spousal* IRA contributions even though his wife didn't have employment income at this time.

- He didn't think he needed to apply for Medicare since he was still working. But you still need to apply for Part A and defer the other Medicare coverage. Unfortunately, he'll be hit with a 10 percent penalty for every year beyond sixty-five he didn't enroll. The penalty never goes away, and he'll be paying the higher premiums for the rest of his life. Fortunately, we got him enrolled immediately to avoid an even costlier penalty.

- They had way too much—about half a million dollars— sitting in a checking/savings account earning less than 0.25

percent interest. We decided on a lower checking/savings amount that would still provide enough liquid cash reserves to make Barbara feel comfortable, and we invested the rest in an appropriate portfolio of diversified, low-cost mutual funds that would generate a much better return than a quarter of a percent.

- Terrence had expensive annuities within an IRA. While I'm rarely an advocate for annuities, I especially don't like them for IRAs. It typically doesn't make sense because you already have tax deferral in an IRA. We were able to transfer these IRA annuities into regular IRAs and reduce his cost by 2.7 percent per year, while also providing a much better selection of investment choices.

- One of Barbara and Terrence's stated priorities was creating a college fund for their six young grandchildren, yet they were saving for this future expense in a regular checking account. We opened 529 education savings plans, which have special tax advantages.

- They also wanted to make sure their children wouldn't be obligated to take care of them as they aged, but they had inadequate long-term care insurance. We were able to identify a cost-effective long-term care strategy and refer them to a qualified long-term-care insurance professional.

- We also worked with their new CPA to ensure things like SEP-IRA contributions were being included and also established a donor-advised fund with highly appreciated stock to carry out their philanthropic intentions and reap better tax savings.

- Finally, we collaborated with an estate attorney to get their legal documents updated and in good order.

Despite having both an advisor and a CPA, none of these things had ever been discussed until they sat down with me. Ultimately, we've netted this couple several hundred thousand dollars over the past several years by reducing expenses, penalties, and taxes and investing according to a low-cost, evidence-based approach.

> Just because someone has "Financial Advisor" on their business card does not necessarily mean they know a lot about either finance or advising.

Heed this warning, because it can save you and your family millions: just because someone has "Financial Advisor" on their business card does not necessarily mean they know a lot about either finance or advising. The industry has many consummate professionals who work hard for their clients, but swimming among them there are sharks, charlatans, and crooks, as well as those who simply aren't qualified to manage and grow large portfolios.

WHAT YOU DON'T KNOW CAN KILL YOUR PORTFOLIO

In life, the path we end up on is rarely the one on which we first set out. Before I became an advisor, my dream was to be a professional baseball player. I had played ball throughout my youth and was good enough to earn a scholarship to the Illinois Institute of Technology (IIT), where I played as a pitcher.

As any serious athlete knows, your chosen sport isn't just a game; it's a way of life. It becomes your identity. And you learn that, notwithstanding the role of genetically induced "natural talent," you're only as good as the effort you put in to being the best. Ultimately, you're judged on little other than your on-field performance.

In this respect, athletics is a true meritocracy: the winnings are there for the taking, but only if you're willing to work harder than your opponent. So you throw yourself headlong into getting better, practicing night and day, lifting weights until your muscles cry out, doing cardio until your body can't move another inch, eating well and practicing discipline at the dinner table even though there's nothing you'd like more right now than another slice of pie. For athletes, sometimes the mental and physical exhaustion feels like it will break you, but what keeps you going is the will to do better, to *be* better. And come game day, the effort you've expended will hopefully pay dividends.

Unfortunately, I learned, the wealth management industry doesn't work the way things do on the diamond. There isn't a level playing field where everyone plays by the same rules and where natural talent crystallizes with hard work and sheer will to produce success. Nor is talent recognized or rewarded equitably. In fact, the "best" advisors—meaning those who reap the most benefits for their clients—are often compensated less than their sales-driven peers, who are judged by how much money they bring in to the firm (not to the client). If that seems like an odd disconnect, well, it is. But often, what is profitable for the brokerage is not so advantageous for the investor. The industry is structurally flawed because in many cases it incentivizes questionable behavior, and it's flawed on the individual level because many advisors themselves are, frankly, subpar.

Below are the major problems with the industry:

1. LOW BARRIER TO ENTRY

It may surprise you to learn that it's not particularly hard to get a job as a "financial advisor" or "wealth manager."

Some advisors might not even have a college degree. It isn't like law, where you have to attend three grueling years of school and then pass the bar, or medicine (even more years of school, followed by rigorous training and tough medical boards).

In our industry, people are often hired not because of their financial acuity or intellectual prowess but because they're good salespeople who can bring in revenue for the firm.

Consider that only 25 percent of people working in my industry have actually earned the gold standard of Certified Financial Planner certification, which is typically a three-year process. At TFA, we require all our advisors to have earned this credential before working directly with clients and providing financial planning and investment advice.

Some advisors whose parents were or are in the industry benefit from nepotism and never had to work hard to gain the trust of clients by demonstrating their own skill set. Others have a checkered track record of compliance issues, yet investors very rarely look into an advisor's history—even though that's public information, thanks to FINRA's Bro-kerCheck, which provides a background check on brokers or anyone affiliated with a broker or dealer. This will show their employment history; securities exams they've passed; where the individual is licensed to do business; and any "disclosure events," which include customer complaints, bankruptcies, DUIs, felonies, and any penalties or fines the broker or their respective firm had to pay.

The US Securities and Exchange Commission (SEC) also administers an advisor search that provides similar background info on investment advisor representatives: people like me who are fee only and not affiliated with broker-dealer firms.[4] But few investors avail themselves of the opportunity to consult these databases.

2. GREEDY, SALES-DRIVEN INDUSTRY

An advisor's role should be fiduciary in nature—that means always doing what is in the best interest of the client, even if it means a lighter paycheck for the advisor. However, the industry is riddled with conflicts of interest between the advisor's bonus and the investor's future. In many firms, generating revenue is priority number one.

A pervasive example of this is the predilection of advisors for pushing annuities on clients even though they are frequently a poor choice. Unscrupulous advisors like them because annuities earn the advisor a generous bonus, usually between 6 and 10 percent of the total value—but now the investor has to lock up their money for years or decades in an asset plagued with confusing surrender schedules, complex rules, and unimpressive returns.

And often, advisors use fear to sell subpar products: "Man, this bull market has been incredible for the last ten years, but the next recession is just around the corner, so we need to protect your money in an annuity. If you do that, you can't lose." And if the client resists, the advisor will lay on the fear even thicker—"Your daughter is going off to college in a couple years. You don't want her future

---

4   For the SEC's advisor search, visit https://www.sec.gov/
     check-your-investment-professional.

jeopardized because your savings have disappeared in the next market crash, do you?" Meanwhile, as the client is browbeaten into a bad decision, the unscrupulous advisor is fantasizing about how he's going to spend his 10 percent commission.

In truth, it's something of a "don't hate the player, hate the game" problem: the aggressive sales culture of these companies makes it very difficult for advisors to survive, let alone take good care of their clients. This is especially true for young employees, who face tremendous pressure to win new business and hit their goals and targets. Rather than tending to the needs of existing clients, you are constantly trying to win new ones.

3. INCESTUOUS BACK-SCRATCHING

Brokerage firms operate revenue sharing agreements with mutual funds and insurance companies to whom they pay kickbacks. It's a "pay-to-play" system, so advisors sell the investment products of companies that are willing to share their revenue with the brokerage firm. In this arrangement, everyone wins but you, the investor.

That also means many of the best investment options (like the well-regarded Dimensional Fund Advisors) are not even available at the biggest firms, and if they are, they come at a higher price than what you would pay using a firm like TFA. The big brokerage firms constantly tout their "open architecture" investment platform, but despite their gargantuan size, the options for the investor are limited. Few investors know this, to their detriment.

4. INADEQUATE REGULATION

All these shortcomings paint a picture of an industry in dire need of government regulation to protect the consumer, but Wall Street and the insurance lobbies have Congress and the White House safely in their pocket. These lobbies stymie any new rules that would address conflicts of interest or compel brokerage firms and individual advisors to act in the interest of their clients.

> All these shortcomings paint a picture of an industry in dire need of government regulation to protect the consumer, but Wall Street and the insurance lobbies have Congress and the White House safely in their pocket.

As an example, consider the dearly departed "fiduciary rule," which required retirement advisors to put their clients' interests before their own—until the US Department of Labor (DOL) shelved the rule in 2017, much to the delight of industry lobbyists. In 2018 the Fifth Circuit Court of Appeals dealt the final death blow to the rule. More recently, as of this writing, there is talk between the DOL and the SEC of reviving the fiduciary rule, but no doubt industry special interests will fight it every step of the way.

A similar controversy involves the SEC's "Regulation Best Interest" guidelines, which, like the DOL fiduciary rule, would require "a broker-dealer … to act in the best interest of a retail customer when making a recommendation of any securities transaction or investment strategy involving securities to a retail customer."[5] The National Association of Insurance and Financial Advisors, the American Council of Life Insurers, the Financial Services Institute, and the Securities Industry and Financial Markets Association oppose the SEC's proposal in the courts and in Congress.[6]

Unfortunately, the power of Wall Street special interests and lobbyists has managed to squelch consumer-friendly legislation and administrative law for a long time, irrespective of which party controls Congress or who happens to occupy the White House at the time.

While we wait for Washington to catch up, the easiest fix would simply be to change the title on one's business card. If you work at Morgan Stanley or Wells Fargo, call yourself a salesperson, not a financial advisor or wealth manager. There's nothing wrong with salespeople. But by concealing with favorable titles the true dynamic of their business, they obscure the conflicts of interest underpinning their work.

5. THE "BROKER CAROUSEL"

Ever wonder why your broker went from Morgan Stanley to Merrill Lynch? And then after five or ten years, they jumped ship again and joined UBS? Top brokers reap tremendous financial rewards as an incentive to move to a

---

5   "SEC Proposes to Enhance Protections and Preserve Choice for Retail Investors in Their Relationships with Investment Professionals," Securities and Exchange Commission, April 18, 2018, https://www.sec.gov/news/press-release/2018-68.

6   Jim Probasco, "Next Target for Lobbyists: SEC Best Interest Rule," Investopedia, July 10, 2018, https://www.investopedia.com/news/next-target-lobbyists-sec-best-interest-rule-0/.

new company, sometimes over 300 percent of their trailing twelve-month revenue. That means a broker who does $5 million in revenue for Merrill Lynch could move to one of the competitors (Morgan Stanley, Stifel, Raymond James, etc.) and garner a $15 million bonus in the process.

Clients rarely benefit from this arrangement. The broker will usually claim that the new firm is much better and can provide an array of new products and options the old firm couldn't (which makes one wonder, if the old firm was so inadequate, why was the broker always touting it?). The reality is that there is very little difference between major firms.

I've seen brokers who have made this lucrative leap four to five times during their careers, dragging along in their wake confused, hapless clients who only want stability and gain nothing when their trusted advisor moves to a completely new company.

DO THE RIGHT THING, EVEN WHEN YOU DON'T HAVE TO

When my daughter, Havana, was born prematurely, it was the most trying, gut-wrenching, soul-searching time of my life. But my first major family crisis happened about ten years before that, when I was still in college and my mother was diagnosed with breast cancer. Not only was her sudden inability to work a major financial blow for our family, but the emotional toll of facing the possible death of a parent was devastating. I'm the youngest in our family, and my mother had always tried to protect me. Now she was the one who needed me.

During this tumultuous period, I was finishing my MBA and using a fifth year of eligibility to play baseball at IIT while working at the Chicago Mercantile Exchange and moonlighting as a bouncer at one of the city's busiest nightclubs. I wanted to keep myself busy to reduce the anxiety over my mother's illness and also be more financially self-sufficient. Dreams of being a professional baseball pitcher were fading thanks to a bum elbow, but I was enjoying studying the financial markets and working out a plan B.

One night at the nightclub, I had a chance encounter with a financial advisor who also happened to be a partner at a brokerage firm. His name was Bob Yarosz, and after a few too many cocktails, he gave me his business card and told me to give him a call if I wanted a job. He was stunned when I called him first thing Monday morning asking for an interview.

I put on my only suit and drove to his office in my beat-up Ford Escort with its cracked windshield and bungee-corded front hood, not quite knowing what to expect. I didn't have a long resume or years of experience, but I did have ambition and a willingness to learn and work hard.

When I met with Bob, he said, "You got the job, kid. I still can't believe you had the guts to call me." Bob would prove to be a great mentor for my early years in the industry, and I'm happy to say we are still friends today. One of the things he always said was, "Do the right thing, even if you don't have to." That resonated strongly with me because that was also how my parents raised me, and I wanted to follow that mantra in my work.

I stayed in Chicago for five years postgraduation, working at Bob's small financial planning and investment firm. During this time, my mom stoically traveled the long road to recovery until she beat cancer. Eventually I moved to North Carolina, where my parents later joined me too, and in 2011, I started my own firm. The next year I merged my business with TFA, and that's where I am today.

In my trajectory from twenty-two-year-old kid in an ill-fitting suit to the CEO and sole owner of a renowned, twenty-person registered investment advisory firm, I didn't take any shortcuts, and I didn't inherit anything. Nobody gave me a playbook to be successful in this industry. I just wanted to outwork my competitors because I believe in meritocracy, and I serve my clients because I believe in integrity. That's the way I was raised.

I believe investors deserve a better experience with financial advisors. I've worked in all the sales channels in this industry (independent broker-dealer model, bank model, wire-house model, and now fee-only registered investment advisor), and I've distilled this diverse experience into a set of best practices that forms the core of TFA, which emphasizes a client-centered, fiduciary approach and a culture that values taking care of employees and actively supporting the community.

My point is not to scare you away from working with an advisor but to arm you with the knowledge about how the industry operates so you can separate the wheat from the chaff to find an advisor who really cares—the type who always does the right thing, even when they don't have to.

TAKEAWAYS:

1. The title "financial advisor" means nothing without the experience, expertise, and ethics to back it up. Ideally, an advisor should also have a CFP® after their name.

2. There are a lot of questionable industry practices that go on behind the scenes that investors never see. Be aware of this fact; even better, don't be afraid to ask your advisor pointed questions about the commissions they receive from selling products or whether the firm has pay-to-play arrangements with mutual fund and insurance companies.

3. As Terrence and Barbara's experience shows, advisors and CPAs falter when they don't look at the total picture of your finances—not just investment but taxation, healthcare or Medicare, charitable giving, and so on.

CHAPTER THREE

YOUR FINANCIAL PLAN

Mary was the kind of student every teacher loves to have in the classroom. Smart, attentive, and eager to learn, she brightened each class with her sunny disposition and made an impression on me from day one. Maybe I made an impression on her too, since after she completed my seminar, she and her husband, Pete, signed on as clients.

Though Mary was married, she attended the class solo. At the time she was in her sixties, but it's never too late to learn about personal finance. In fact, most of my students are baby boomers. Mary had spent several decades in the workforce, had been saving all her life, and knew a fair bit about investment, but the concept of financial planning was still new to her.

Since it was the second marriage for both Mary and Pete, they kept a lot of their financial matters separate, and Pete preferred to take a do-it-yourself approach to managing his money. They say that men are less inclined to ask for help—we've all heard the old joke about the wife imploring her hopelessly lost husband to pull over and ask for directions. In my experience as an instructor and an advisor, there seems to be some truth to that.

Mary's decision to educate herself about financial planning proved sadly prudent a few years later, when Pete died at the relatively young age of sixty-three. One of the big truths of my line of work, a lesson I strive to pass on to my clients and students, is that anything can happen to anyone at any time. We can't control or prevent that. All we can do is be prepared.

I attended Pete's service and was amazed by the number of people who were celebrating his life. From the stories that were told and from a touching video of Mary and Pete's life together, it was obvious that they were extremely close and deeply in love. My eyes were watering just knowing what a devastating loss this was for her.

As anyone who has been through a similar misfortune knows, losing a spouse, parent, or other close relative brings a sudden onslaught of logistical and financial challenges, exactly at the time when grief leaves you least able to handle them. When Pete died, Mary faced several of these problems. She would now have to face the future on her own, managing her money and providing for herself with no one to support her. And she had to handle the estate of a blended family, since this was the second marriage for both of them and they both had children from their previous marriages. (Fortunately, a properly designed estate plan unambiguously stipulated how Pete intended his assets to pass upon his death.)

It's times like these when the value of financial planning becomes clear. You don't know what you don't know, I often say, so that means you have to consider all possible contingencies ahead of time, lest you're caught off guard. A solid financial plan will carry you through tough times. And that's critical, because for almost all of us, sooner or later a crisis or tragedy will occur.

Today, ten years after she walked into my classroom, Mary is happy, healthy, and in excellent financial shape. She remains one of my most loyal clients, and she tells me to this day that one of the best decisions she ever made was enrolling in that seminar, which taught her what she needed to know to move forward and be able to take care of herself no matter what. During the awful period after her husband's passing, her confidence was put to the test, but she stuck to the plan and handled the onslaught of new challenges capably.

A financial plan isn't just there to prepare for hard times; it's for *all times*. It provides clarity and a road map for the long term. Perhaps you want to better manage your finances, but you're not sure where to start. Or maybe you have an immediate need: you lost your job, lost a spouse, inherited money, are going through a divorce, are selling a business, are interested in funding a college education, or are caring for aging parents or an adult child who isn't yet financially independent. With a financial plan, you can navigate all these life events and make important decisions with confidence.

> A financial plan isn't just there to prepare for hard times; it's for all times.

At TFA, we take a comprehensive approach to planning that looks at your complete financial picture. Investing is a big part of it, but it also encompasses healthcare, insurance, estate planning, taxation, and charitable giving. In fact, with new clients, we don't even talk about investing until there's a plan in place. Investment strategy and financial planning go hand in hand and are interdependent. That dual emphasis is one of the hallmarks of our approach to building wealth and a major contributor to our clients' success over the years.

But it all starts with one simple question: What do you want from life?

GAME ON: SETTING GOALS, LIVING WITH INTENTION

Financial planning is goal oriented—each plan is engineered to meet each of your short-, intermediate-, and long-term goals according to a predefined timeline. Figuring out goals is easier said than done, since many people never really sit down and think hard about what they want from life. Sure, everyone has vaguely defined goals: "I want to be happy" or "I want to have enough money for retirement." Well, I would hope so! Very few of us strive to be too poor to retire. But financial planning means mulling over your objectives in a more methodical, concrete sense.

To kick-start the planning process, we've developed our own board game to help individuals and couples articulate and prioritize their goals. The game is called "Intentions," which also happens to be the guiding philosophy of everything we do at TFA. To be *intentional* is to live and act with purpose, direction, and vision. It's dangerously easy to drift through life willy-nilly, without keeping an eye fixed on the onrushing future. Then, before you know it, ten, fifteen, twenty years have gone by, and you wonder what happened and what you've been doing all that time. Or maybe a crisis—job loss, illness, debt—rears its ugly head, and you're unsure how to respond. Intentionality is essential for living a happy and healthy life and armors you against unforeseen problems and aimless existence. COVID-19 is a perfect example. As people have been thrust into a pandemic that has jeopardized not only their health but their jobs and financial independence, they need to take a hard look at their goals and what's really important to them going forward.

It's heavy stuff that might not seem to lend itself to something fun like a board game, but clients love the experience, and they learn a lot from it.

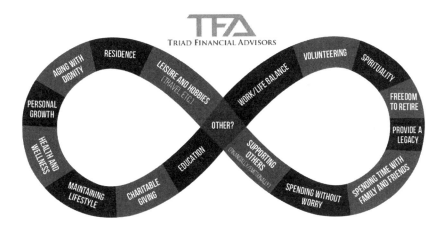

Basically, the board is a visual representation of common goals, things like "education" or "income security" or "aging with dignity" or "protecting my family." The players are given a set of chips, and they go around the board and place chips on different spaces in accord with their priorities. There's a limited number of chips, which forces people to make compromises and think hard about what really matters to them.

The game is a powerful conversation starter, especially between spouses—spouses talk about anything and everything from the weather to vexing philosophical questions to "Has this mole always been here?" but sometimes they go years without discussing the fundamental question of "What do we want from life, and how do we get it?"

The game is an excellent starting point for the client-advisor relationship, which thrives on mutual understanding and candor. Observing people play Intentions tells me a lot about their personalities and what they desire from life. A good advisor gets to know his clients on a much deeper level than just how much is in their 401(k)s and which deductions they take on their tax returns.

Playing Intentions is not always a lighthearted, casual experience. Sometimes the game can elicit raw emotions, since financial planning requires engaging with pretty serious, life-and-death stuff. Plenty of people end up spilling their guts during the process. It gets emotional, and that can be hard. But honesty and introspection lead to better conversations, which are the seed of better planning.

For example, I had one recent eye-opening session with a new client. She had just inherited a huge amount of money from her recently deceased father, and she needed some advice. When we crunched the numbers, it was clear that, with the inheritance, she'd be set for life. She could quit working and enjoy a luxurious retirement if she wanted; she could do almost anything with all that money.

But she wasn't thrilled. In fact, she seemed deeply upset by it. "I don't deserve this money," she said. "This isn't mine. This was my dad's that he worked so hard for. My parents never took vacations and never spent or splurged on anything. And now all of a sudden he's passed all of this on to me. It wouldn't be right for me to go and spend this money on myself, when my dad and mom never indulged themselves."

This triggered an emotional conversation as she recounted the story of her upbringing, when it felt like they never had enough money when in actuality it was because her folks, Depression-era kids who knew the value of scrimping and saving, had been squirreling funds away while living extremely frugally.

That experience sharpened my psychological acuity as an advisor by making me think more deeply about people's motivations, which aren't always simple or intuitive. Every person comes into my office with a unique set of experiences, values, wants, needs, fears, hopes, and desires. Consequently, you can give five people a million dollars each, and they're all going to respond to it in myriad ways. Each financial plan must account for these emotional and personal nuances.

BUILDING A PLAN THAT LASTS

The development of the plan follows this process:

1. Establishing a relationship with a CFP® like me who outlines the CFP®'s services and responsibilities as well as how they are compensated. At TFA, we work on a fee-only basis, which minimizes conflicts of interest arising from more commission-oriented compensation schemes.

2. Identifying financial and life goals—having candid conversations about what money means to people and how their finances will enable or inhibit the pursuit of their goals and values.

3. Collecting financial data: assets (401(k)s, IRAs, brokerage accounts, savings/money markets, home, rental properties, annuities, 529 plans, health savings accounts, etc.); liabilities (mortgage, vehicle loans, credit card debt, lines of credit, etc.); cash flow (income and expenses); pensions; Social

Security income; tax returns; estate planning documents; insurance in-force as well as cash value, if any; how much they are saving each pay period; and how much they spend monthly and annually.

There's so much data that needs to be gathered, as the plan is only as good as the data fed into it. Unfortunately, this is where a lot of people procrastinate or lose interest because consolidating that mountain of paperwork can be tedious, if not altogether overwhelming. It's a bit like getting undressed in front of a doctor for a physical! (At least you don't have to "turn your head and cough.")

1. The CFP® then analyzes the current assets, liabilities, cash flow, insurance coverage, investments, tax strategies, and estate plan.

2. The CFP® develops and presents recommendations and/or alternatives.

3. We then implement the plan.

4. Once the financial plan is in place, the work isn't done. It needs to be continuously revisited to make sure you stay on track and make adjustments as needed and as life happens.

Unfortunately, there are a lot of subpar financial plans done by people in the industry. One of the most common mistakes involves making unrealistically rosy projections about investment returns over a long timeline. Advisors often project generous returns throughout the life of the plan with minimal volatility, but the market doesn't generate 10 percent returns year after year without any volatility. And when you're retired, when you combine downside volatility in the markets with distributions from the portfolio for living expenses, in addition to inflation, it can change a financial plan dramatically.

We want to use capital market assumptions that reflect reasonable estimates for the next twenty, thirty, or forty years. With a relatively flat yield curve and interest rates close to zero, it's simply not prudent to expect the same rates of return from fixed income that investors have earned over the past forty years.

Furthermore, many advisors tend to underestimate life expectancy. Affluent people tend to live longer, healthier lives, so we always want to assume our clients live considerably longer than the average male or female. Underestimating a client's life span can throw the whole plan out of whack.

Another key question is how much cash you should keep in cash and how much you should save into money markets. We design the plan around a ten-year cash need analysis, with an eye toward allowing you to draw a paycheck from your portfolio in retirement (the subject of chapter 6).

As for how much to hold in cash, in my experience retirees seem to be a lot happier if they have more liquid cash ready for any type of situation, regardless of how much money they also have in their IRAs and brokerage accounts. Some clients prefer to hold $100,000 in a low-interest savings account because it gives them peace of mind. If that makes them happier, that's fine (as long as they have all their ducks in a row). It's just one of those emotional things that you must accommodate as an advisor.

This ability to listen to our clients and not just follow a playbook helped tremendously during the COVID-19 pandemic. Although still unsettled with portfolio values decreasing, our clients understand they have plenty of cash to meet any emergency needs while we wait for stocks to rebound. Some investors may even look at this as an opportunity to deploy some of that cash into temporarily depressed stock prices.

While we strive to take some of the emotion out of planning and investing, we can't deny how someone feels. Only by being strong listeners can advisors provide an excellent experience for our clients that is mindful of their emotions and desires.

At the same time, we aim to give people what they need, not just what they want. So, if someone feels better keeping large cash reserves, we make sure that that cash is earning the best interest rate possible.

Taxes are another major component of financial planning. Taxes affect you every year of your working life, but they will continue to exert a big influence through the duration of your retirement. Many people don't realize that most forms of retirement income are still subject to federal and state taxation.

Most of our clients are high-net-worth people whose capital is concentrated in their 401(k) plans, and so they've been enjoying tax deductions the entire time they've been putting money in there. But as soon as they start taking money out, it is taxable as ordinary income. It catches people off guard when they planned to have $5,000 a month in cash, only to discover they must withdraw $7,000 to net $5,000 after taxes.

That's just one example of a hundred different tax considerations that we walk through when devising a plan.

Medicare is another huge issue for a lot of people. In the year before turning sixty-five, they're getting bombarded with solicitations about how they need to sign up for Medicare and how they need this or that supplement. Figuring out Medicare can feel like navigating a giant maze. It's something that many financial advisors don't even address in their planning, but at TFA, we have a specialist in house who counsels people on their Medicare options.

Social Security is another area that's fraught with questions. For example, when to start withdrawing? It depends on so many factors involving both you and your spouse that there's no straightforward answer. The COVID-19 pandemic led many to believe they need to start taking their Social Security benefits sooner to meet their income needs instead of waiting for the delayed credits. While that may be a potential solution, you need to develop a "Social Security plan" that gels with the other elements of your plan. That's actually an essential point about all these elements: nothing is addressed in isolation. Every aspect, from investment to healthcare to tax to charitable giving, is a moving component of a complex system. All the pieces must fit together and work in sync to help you realize your goals.

KEEPING THE PLAN UP TO DATE

The plan only works if you keep it fresh by making adjustments as time goes on. Back in the day, advisors would create a detailed financial plan full of assumptions and recommendations that were supposed to last for thirty years. But today, financial planning must be more fluid and flexible. Economic conditions are always in flux, and anyone's life can change radically overnight. The plan must be able to respond to unforeseen personal developments in addition to economic trends. Fortunately, financial planning software allows us to adapt and model changing scenarios relatively easily.

It's a lot like building a home. A well-built house is designed to stand for decades or more, but you still need to make repairs and upgrades over time to keep it aesthetically appealing and structurally durable. So it goes with the financial plan: sturdy enough at the core to form the foundation of your financial life for many years, but flexible and adaptable enough to be refreshed, retooled, and refined at the margins.

There isn't a fixed schedule for updating plans. At TFA, we'll usually do it every six or twelve months; sometimes, it's every time a client comes in. As we do the update, we take stock of progress and evaluate whether we're on track with helping clients meet their goals and manage their expenses.

Recently, I met with a pair of clients (a married couple) who had for a long time been planning to live in a continuing care retirement community when they turned eighty. Continuing care is an expensive endeavor that requires a lot of money and advance planning to make it happen.

During the meeting, they announced that although they were still seven years shy of their target age, they were both ready to move into the continuing care facility. Seven extra years of increased living expenses to pay for the facility would significantly alter the financial plan, so we had to rerun all the numbers to make sure all those projections still made sense. Fortunately, because we had developed an airtight plan and had stuck to it for years, my clients had enough of a cushion to make it work. It's probably cliché to say, but it bears repeating: planning gives you peace of mind. It helps you avoid scrambling when your needs or circumstances change. Remember— you don't know what you don't know!

Modifying the plan may also require modifying your own lifestyle by making sacrifices and trade-offs. Two of my clients are a married couple who are now retired. Before they retired, he had been employed by a big tobacco company for years, but when they unexpectedly let him go, he had to find a challenge and sense of purpose in his life. You're never too old to reinvent yourself, and the man found success and satisfaction by starting a business around his lifelong passion of croquet. Now he was teaching the sport and organizing tournaments. The major drawback was that the new venture kept him in Florida for much of the year, away from his wife in North Carolina. They both wanted her to be able to retire so that she could join him there; they missed being together, and she wanted time with grandkids that she couldn't get working forty hours a week. But they still needed her income since they hadn't met all their financial goals yet.

Even if you're well off, sometimes competing interests in your plan require you to make trade-offs: you give up one thing to enjoy more of another. In this case, the couple and I found ways they could trim their budget and simplify their lifestyle. So instead of renting a villa in St. Barts that year, they spent their holidays in a little condo in the Florida Keys. Instead of holding on to their vacation home in North Carolina throughout their retirement, they agreed to sell it. In truth, the house had become something of a burden. It was unoccupied eight months out of the year, and maintenance, upkeep, insurance, and taxes offset the minimal gains from renting it out a few weeks a year as a vacation property. This way, they could rid themselves of the responsibility of an underperforming asset while adding the value of the sale of the property to their portfolio. Ultimately, by incorporating some belt-tightening into the plan, we found a way to let her retire early.

These steps weren't part of the original plan, but as the couple considered their later-in-life priorities—above all, being together—they made adjustments. Today, they're quite happy croqueting all over the Sunshine State and living comfortably despite the cutbacks. He was even inducted into the US Croquet Hall of Fame. Who knew such a thing even existed?

It worked out for them, but in other cases, the numbers just don't allow for major deviations from the plan, especially with respect to early retirement. People who have been working for decades turn sixty, sixty-one, sixty-two, maybe they see some of their friends retire or they're just done with the daily grind, and they decide they're ready to move on to the next phase of their life.

Dan was one of those people. Dan and Lisa, like the aforementioned couple, had to switch gears suddenly when Dan was laid off. He was still a few years from retirement, but he was *done*. He had no interest in returning to work or starting a new career at a different company. Lisa, meanwhile, was still gainfully employed and willing to work as long as she was healthy.

As we discussed their future together, Dan told me that with Lisa's earnings, plus his Social Security, he was confident they would be okay. But we ran the numbers, and it didn't look good. I didn't feel comfortable telling him he didn't have to work anymore.

Plus, as the three of us mulled over the calculations, I could see that Lisa was scared out of her mind. But she didn't seem to want to tell her husband to go back to work either. There was a lot of tension in the room.

My job as an advisor is not to tell people what to do but to speak candidly, provide them with all possible options, and advise accordingly. I had to give it to him straight. "Sorry, Dan, but this just isn't gonna work. I think you're going to have to continue to do something. At least part-time work, consulting, anything." From the angry glare he directed at me, it was evident he wasn't happy with that suggestion. And that was the end of that meeting.

But in the weeks that followed, Lisa privately expressed her gratitude for breaking the hard news and working with them on an alternate plan. Eventually, they came back in, and Dan accepted the reality of his situation and found part-time work. It wasn't plan A, but it let them continue to live the life they wanted.

Wake-up calls like that are just part of the business. It's not enough to look at your portfolio and see that you have $1 or $2 million saved and assume that you and your spouse are good for the next forty years of postwork life. It's only when you actually start running all the numbers, considering all factors and expenses, examining all the different consequences that might arise, and accounting for projected market volatility and other unknowns that you get a firm answer about the viability of your retirement.

One of the biggest questions we get is "Do I stick to the plan during a market crash?" One of the advantages of having a comprehensive financial plan is that you can model different scenarios and illustrate what would happen in very volatile times—if a 20 or 30 percent downturn in the market decimated your portfolio, how would that affect your intermediate- and long-term prospects?

No one can accurately predict the future, but now the technology is advanced to a degree that we can walk the client through various situations and study closely how future events might affect their lifestyle.

However, the most sensitive part of the plan does not necessarily involve lower-than-expected returns. It's more a question of spending. And of course, unless you happen to be the chairman of the Fed, you exert much more control over your own spending than you do on market performance.

One-off splurges like a luxury car will rarely sidetrack your plan, but when spending rises over the long term, or when you sink a very large amount of capital into a new asset (like a second home), we have to revisit the plan and see if there are ways to cut back. Housing and auto expenses usually constitute the biggest chunk of personal expenses. Travel is another one, especially for people in their earlier retirement years, when they're in better physical and mental condition to venture far afield. So travel is often the first area where I prescribe some belt-tightening. Instead of a $20,000 Viking Caribbean cruise each year, maybe go with renting a beach condo for a week.

That said, if amazing travel and experiences are really important, we just need to work with the client to prioritize and help them understand a splurge in one area might require a sacrifice in another. If you want the second home, then perhaps the cruise won't be in the budget. However, if you forgo the second home, you will probably enjoy a bigger budget for expensive travel.

It's not just discretionary expenditures that can arise. Spikes in spending also result from (unforeseeable) life events, like helping a child who is going through a divorce and needs a lot of financial support, or caring for aging parents.

In these cases, the extra expenses are unavoidable and usually inflexible, but the response is the same: we go back to the plan and pull different levers to compensate. If you're still employed, there are more options to handle such challenges. Maybe it means working a few more years before retiring. Maybe it means getting a little bit more aggressive in the portfolio to generate the probability of better returns over time.

For people who are already retired or on the verge of retirement and who can't take on more portfolio risk or return to work, there are still options. You start by going back to the drawing board (or the game board, as it were) and reevaluating your priorities again: if your priority is to help your kids buy a new home or put your elderly parents in nursing care, then we'll work to help you cut back on some of your own discretionary spending. There's always another lever to pull, always some way to tug on the loose ends and give some extra slack.

MONEY: THE MEANS, NOT THE END

Wealth is about living the way you want. It's not merely a number in terms of dollars and assets; it's about having choices.

When we first started using the Intentions game, what struck me was how infrequently people named "being rich" as their first priority. Usually it's physical and cognitive health that top the list. Without your health, none of this money matters. You could afford an extravagant trip around the world—twice—but if you're not able-bodied or of sound mind, you won't get much farther than your own driveway. And if you don't have strong social relations and familial bonds to keep you rooted

> Money alone can't make you happy, but it certainly provides the resources to let you pursue happiness on your terms. It's a tool that can be used to build the metaphorical dream house of your life.

and friends and family to share in your joy, then even lavish wealth can feel lackluster, like something is missing.

Money alone can't make you happy, but it certainly provides the *resources* to let you pursue happiness on your terms. It's a tool that can be used to build the metaphorical dream house of your life.

My dad was a working man, and when he heard someone more affluent complaining about all the taxes they had to pay, he used to joke, "Well, let me earn what you do, and then I'll worry about the taxes!" It was a quip that half-kiddingly suggested, "If I were rich, all my problems would be taken care of." But I see that our happiest clients are not necessarily the wealthiest but the ones who are intentional about everything they do. Money helps them get where they want to go, but it isn't the aim itself.

And having enough money to have choices—to be the one who decides, rather than letting the world decide for you—depends on sound planning that encompasses the totality of one's financial life. It requires realistic projections about investment returns and longevity, responsible spending habits, and a prudent investment strategy. It demands a long-term, slow-and-steady-wins-the-race mindset with enough give to let you enjoy life in the short term too.

And that is how you win the game.

KEY QUESTIONS:

1. *If budgeting becomes necessary later in life, what categories of discretionary spending should I target first?*

2. *How should I respond to swings in the market? Or should I just stay the course and wait for volatility to pass?*

3. *What do I do if a sudden major expense—one that can't be avoided, like caring for an ailing relative—affects my retirement?*

4. *What are the things (family, health, freedom, intellectual stimulation, etc.) that matter most to me now? What will I need to remain happy in retirement? In ten years? In twenty? In thirty?*

TAKEAWAYS:

1. Financial planning is a lot more than just investing. It's a system of many moving parts, interlocking and interdependent. A good advisor addresses them all in a single plan.

2. What usually derails a plan is not volatility in the market but excessive spending. Minimizing the latter lets you weather the former.

3. Work, live, and plan with intention. Like a beacon, intention will keep you on a straight path toward your goals and help to illuminate your life priorities.

4. People often talk about getting emotion out of the equation when it comes to personal finance. But that's only half-true. Emotion is a factor that must be considered, since emotion—how you feel—is the heart of personal well-being, and that's what we're working toward, not just numbers on a spreadsheet.

CHAPTER FOUR

EVIDENCE-BASED INVESTING

When it comes to investing, keep it simple, stupid! Don't make it more difficult than it has to be, and you'll be handsomely rewarded come retirement.

Evidence-based investing takes a rational, scientific approach to the thorny question of where to put your money to best make it work for you. It seeks to take human emotion and intellectual guesswork out of the equation by examining long-term historical trends and buying and holding a well-balanced, globally diversified portfolio composed of asset classes that have performed well over time.

Evidence-based investing helps mitigate "fear of missing out" (chasing hot equities at their peak, when it's already too late to buy in) and panic selling (dumping shares at the exact moment when they're careening toward the bottom). These are fear-based decisions that cause investors to buy high and sell low, and that kind of emotionally driven trading will eat away at your portfolio over time. In that sense, evidence-based investing protects you from yourself. We're all only human, after all.

Rather than fighting markets by trying to pick stocks or guess when market highs and lows will occur (an almost impossible task to do consistently), evidence-based investing emphasizes letting the market work *for* you. Though the market undergoes periods of volatility, it trends up over the long term. Buy strong equities and hold them for a long time. That's the main thrust.

There are innumerable variables that influence market behavior, but four patterns stand out in particular, and we can use these to our advantage:

1. **The stock market will outperform the bond market over time.** On average, stocks generate returns of around 10 percent and bonds between 5 and 6 percent.[7]

2. **Small companies outperform large companies over time.** In US markets, over ten-year periods, small beat large 73 percent of the time (based on data from 1927–2018).[8]

3. **Value stocks outperform growth stocks over time.** Growth stocks tend to do better in bull markets, but in down markets, and in the long term overall, value investing has the edge.[9] From July 1926–December 2018, value stocks

---

7   CNN Money, "How do bond returns compare with stock returns?" https://money.cnn.com/retirement/guide/investing_bonds.moneymag/index3.htm.

8   Based on information provided by Dimensional Fund Advisors.

9   Ryan Ermey, "Value vs. Growth Stocks: Which Will Come Out on Top?" *Kiplinger's Personal Finance*, August 2, 2018, https://www.kiplinger.com/

beat growth stocks 83 percent of the time in ten-year rolling periods.

4. **Higher-profitability firms outperform lower-profitability firms over time.** This one is particularly striking because even in one-year time periods (using data from US markets from 1963 to 2018), high-profitability firms outdid their counterparts 67 percent of the time, and over ten-year periods, 99 percent of the time.[10]

Note that we still aim for *outperformance*. We're not merely trying to match the market, which is the very definition of mediocrity. If that was our goal, we'd just buy an index fund and call it a day. Instead, we're pursuing a strategy that calibrates the right risk-reward ratio to produce the highest return, with an eye toward long-term (rather than short- or intermediate-term) gains. We can be confident in that approach because decades of historical data back it up. It's a proven philosophy that increases the probability of outperforming the market, if you're disciplined enough to stick with it.

DIMENSIONAL FUND ADVISORS: THE FINANCIAL SERVICES INDUSTRY'S BEST-KEPT SECRET

Evan has been a client of mine for about five years. When we first started working together, his portfolio was a mess, since his capital was spread out over twenty different actively managed, expensive (high-fee) funds. The average investor does not need so many different funds. Worse, there was still a lot of overlap between these

---

article/investing/T052-C000-S002-value-vs-growth-stocks-which-will-come-out-on-top.html.

10 Based on information provided by Dimensional Fund Advisors.

many funds, so he wasn't even properly diversified. He was invested heavily in US stocks with almost no exposure to the international market, and he was almost exclusively focused on large-cap stocks, thus missing out on the higher upside potential of small caps.

I consolidated his twenty different funds down to seven, which actually ended up *increasing* his portfolio diversification while cutting fees by about 40 percent. Going forward, Evan has been in a position where he has a higher probability of achieving investment success.

It was easy to rebalance Evan's investments thanks to my company's partnership with Dimensional Fund Advisors (DFA), which is one of the most powerful weapons in our wealth-building arsenal. DFA is not a household name like Vanguard or Fidelity, but the company is the seventh biggest mutual fund company in the world, with half a trillion dollars in assets under management. They're not the flashy high roller with the slick suit and the $200 haircut; they're more like the unassuming millionaire next door in T-shirt and jeans. The high roller might have some big years here and there, but he lacks staying power; his methods don't pan out over the long run. The DFA type is methodical, bookish, and quiet, but he earns solid returns decade to decade, getting methodically, bookishly, quietly rich.

DFA flies under the radar, but its years of success speak for themselves. For example, in thirteen different categories of flagship equity funds (from US large cap to international small cap to real estate securities), over a fifteen-year period ending in 2018, DFA outperformed most other funds in all categories.[11] The twenty-year numbers are even more compelling: 83 percent of DFA's equity and

---

11   Dimensional Fund Advisors, "Relative Performance of Flagship Equity Funds," https://switchpointfinancial.com/wp-content/uploads/2018/11/Relative-Performance-of-Flagship-Equity-Funds.pdf.

fixed income funds beat their benchmarks, while only 17 percent of actively managed funds that started in January 1999 outperformed their respective benchmarks.[12]

DFA's philosophy is consistent with the investment strategy we practice at TFA: allowing the historic trends of the market to work for you rather than pursuing the fool's errand of trying to outsmart it; minimizing buying and selling to keep fees down; and maintaining a balanced, globally diversified portfolio consisting of proven assets.

One of the big draws of DFA is its exclusivity—you can invest in their funds through only a small number of select advising firms, like ours. Unlike most of its competitors, DFA doesn't engage in pay-to-play arrangements with big brokerage houses; it also doesn't pay kickbacks to advisors who recommend it. And because it's not marketing to a mass audience of retail investors, it doesn't have huge advertising budgets. These elements all help keep costs down, which means more money in the client's pocket.

DFA owes much of its success to its academic approach to investing. The company draws on empirical research and applies scientific rigor to figuring out how to maximize returns. And it counts several prominent academics—most notably Kenneth French and Nobel laureate Eugene Fama—on its Board of Directors.

The academic underpinnings of DFA enable the company to stay above the fray by avoiding market timing calls, emotional trading, and knee-jerk responses to short-term market conditions. Between the frenetic twenty-four-hour news cycle and the ubiquity of financial media online, investors are constantly pummeled with data. Too much information is counterproductive and creates a lot of emotionally driven noise that can be detrimental to making prudent decisions.

---

12   Based on information provided by Dimensional Fund Advisors.

DFA might be the best-kept secret on Wall Street, because despite its glittering track record, few investors have heard of it. I'd even estimate that four-fifths of *advisors* don't know about it. Instead of getting the word out with traditional marketing channels, the company relies on its stellar reputation and excellent track record. That in itself is a positive sign: a good product or service doesn't need gimmicks, flash, or in-your-face advertising. It sells itself.

It might seem like I'm plugging DFA a little too overtly, but I believe one of the best things I've done for our clientele is establishing our firm's relationship with DFA. It's hard to filter out noise and marketing in the financial services industry, and we are often enchanted by the Wall Street rhetoric of those who pretend to be able to predict the future or who take shortcuts to achieve wealth and security. DFA resonated with me because of the elegant simplicity of its offerings and the truth in many decades of data. Basically, through DFA, we can offer our clients a simple solution to a complex problem, free of conflicts of interest or other funny business. Everyone wins.

WHY DO PEOPLE TRY TO TIME THE MARKET IF THEY'RE SO BAD AT IT?

There's a ton of data that indicates that stock picking and market timing are extremely difficult to do consistently. For example, from 2003 to 2018, only one in thirteen large-cap managers, one in twenty-one mid-cap managers, and one in forty-three small-cap managers exceeded their benchmark index.[13] The evidence for a buy-

---

13   Aye M. Soe and Berlinda Liu, "SPIVA U.S. Scorecard," S&P Dow Jones Indices, https://us.spindices.com/documents/spiva/spiva-us-mid-year-2018.pdf.

and-hold strategy that goes *with* the market rather than trying to outwit it is persuasive.

If hedge fund managers, quants, and other professional investors who spend their whole lives looking at charts and poring over prospectuses can't beat the market consistently, why do so many amateur traders and retail investors keep trying?

It's the same reason people keep going to Vegas to try to score big even though everyone knows that "the house always wins." It's the thrill of the chase, combined with the secret hope we all nurture that we will succeed where almost everyone else has failed. People relish the dopamine hit generated by gambling, whether at the blackjack table or with their brokerage account. And human beings tend to overestimate their abilities—it's easy to convince yourself that with the right amount of pluck, timing, and *Trading for Dummies* books, you can be part of that exclusive elite that trades profitably.

> If hedge fund managers, quants, and other professional investors who spend their whole lives looking at charts and poring over prospectuses can't beat the market consistently, why do so many amateur traders and retail investors keep trying?

I'm not maligning those who salivate at the prospect of a 20X stock pick; I mean, I get it. A DFA-investment style can be a little boring. If trading and stock picking is like a wild weekend at the Bellagio, buying mutual funds is like a day trip to Albany. With your in-laws. Mutual funds are pretty predictable, which makes them uninspiring, and they're unlikely to generate lavishly outsized gains that you would get from the elusive "hot stock tip." However, if you stick to the plan, mutual funds will make you rich eventually, and that's what matters in the end.

Besides the thrill of the chase, people just have a predilection for looking for shortcuts or a free lunch. Passive, buy-and-hold investment will let you build wealth, but it doesn't happen overnight. Call it a "get-rich-slow" scheme. Not everyone has the patience or discipline for that.

The S&P 500 hit an all-time high on February 19, 2020, and investors were still giddy about the eleven-year bull market run. Growth stocks, like the FAANG tech giants (Facebook, Apple, Amazon, Netflix, and Google), have left the traditional value stocks in the dust and looking somewhat lackluster. However, COVID-19 put the global markets into a tailspin, ending the bull market, and this situation has challenged investors. What do you do now? That's when an investment philosophy is really tested—is it strong enough to carry you through good times as well as bad? Decades of stock market performance indicate yes, so the philosophy underpinning evidence-based investing remains intact. In times of uncertainty (which will always exist), I choose to invest alongside those that are going to give me and my clients the greatest probability of having a successful outcome.

A major perk of working with an advisor is that they will act as a

> A major perk of working with an advisor is that they will act as a firewall between you, your brokerage account, and the ups and downs of the market, moderating your emotional reaction to financial vicissitudes.

firewall between you, your brokerage account, and the ups and downs of the market, moderating your emotional reaction to financial vicissitudes. Part of the advisor's role is being the rock to keep you stable through protracted volatility.

The veterans and the people we've worked with for a long time know that they can rest easy in the understanding that we have things covered for them during a recession. However, even the most seasoned investors can be unnerved in volatile markets and start second-guessing their investments and their financial plans. These are the times when a true financial advisor earns their stripes. This is the World Series for my profession! This is where our skills are on full display and we can identify opportunities and provide solutions to clients. We can look to rebalance portfolios (buy low, sell high) to get asset allocations back to their target. We can do tax-loss harvesting in portfolios to realize capital losses that can be used to offset future capital gains. A strong financial advisor can add tremendous value during both good and bad times.

INVESTMENTS TO AVOID

There are a million different ways to invest your money. As an advisor, it's my job to help clients steer their capital to investments that perform well. It's equally important to prevent them from investing in the wrong places. When it comes to the following areas, proceed with caution.

ANNUITIES

We've already touched on why annuities are bad for most investors—and why, despite their drawbacks, so many financial advisors and insurance agents actively push them. Annuities can pay out a fixed annual amount, but if you want to withdraw more than that in the first seven to ten years, you'll typically face significant surrender charges, in addition to other high fees for the duration of the plan.

And with nonqualified annuities, or non-IRA annuities, you do not have a step-up in cost basis upon your death. Let's say I put $1 million into an annuity, which eventually grows to $3 million. If I'm holding that in a normal brokerage account, when I die, I get a step-up in cost basis, so my beneficiaries won't have to pay any capital gains tax. It would get stepped up to $3 million, my date-of-death value, and they could walk away not having to pay any tax on that gain.

However, in an annuity, the step-up in cost basis generally doesn't apply, and gains are not treated as long-term capital gains, so those $2 million in gains would be taxed as ordinary income.

There are a few uncommon cases where an annuity might be advantageous. I think it can be especially useful for people who are elderly and want the assurance of an income stream they can't outlive. Say a seventy-year-old woman invests $500,000 in an annuity. She can withdraw, say, 6 percent of that annually ($30,000) for the rest of her life, even if she lives to be 120 years old, long past the point at which her initial $500,000 investment has been exhausted. The company is still obligated to pay out that $30,000. However, if she dies at eighty-five, the company retains whatever money is left if the annuity contract has been "annuitized."

But for the vast majority of investors, it's not worth it. You're better off putting your money in a low-cost, diversified portfolio of stock and bond mutual funds.

HEDGE FUNDS AND ALTERNATIVE INVESTMENTS

In 2008, Warren Buffett famously made a bet with Ted Seides, cofounder of Protégé Partners, an asset management firm, that a million-dollar investment in a simple index fund that tracks the S&P 500 would outperform a basket of funds chosen by a hedge fund. Ten years later, Seides admitted defeat: the index fund garnered 7 percent returns, while the hand-picked funds generated a measly 2.2 percent.

It wasn't a total blowout. In fact, initially, the hedge fund had the edge as the Great Recession pummeled the stock market. But the ten-year outcome speaks for itself. This just exemplifies that everything reverts to the mean, and short-term or yearly gains are easily eclipsed by the long view.

As an advisor, I urge people to stay away from hedge funds and other alternative investments. The numbers are not in your favor. The financial press loves trumpeting stories of hedge fund managers' extravagant wealth—helicoptering-to-the-Hamptons kind of money. But hedge fund managers are not necessarily rich because they're

> As an advisor, I urge people to stay away from hedge funds and other alternative investments. The numbers are not in your favor.

savvy investors generating stellar returns; they're getting rich because their well-heeled clients foist gobs of money upon them.

The reality is that despite a few rare exceptions, hedge funds underperform your basic, low-cost index stuff and over long time frames drastically lag behind Dimensional Fund Advisors.

REAL ESTATE: WHY BUYING A SECOND HOME IS NOT A GOOD IDEA

Avoid this common trap. Though it seems promising at the time, buying a second home usually just becomes a money suck, and it takes away a lot of flexibility in retirement.

People tend to purchase a second home either as a rental property or a vacation home (which they might also rent for part of the year).

But unless you're in a hot real estate market like California or Seattle or New York, the return on investment is rarely worth the hassle. There are better ways of growing your money.

Investors mistakenly think real estate means guaranteed easy money. I had one client who, over my vehement objections, withdrew all his retirement money (paying early withdrawal penalties and taxes galore) to build a $3 million, 12,000-square-foot home, one of the biggest in Greensboro. He insisted that it would surely pay off in the long run; after all, houses always appreciate, right?

I had to drop him as a client because I couldn't in good faith abide by such an unwise move. The home he constructed was absolutely stunning, inside and out, but I hope he enjoyed it, because financially, it was a major failure. This $3 million investment, which he had put everything on the line for, sold for $1.47 million in bankruptcy.

This is an atypical case, but people tend to overlook the ancillary costs that make owning a second home expensive. Property taxes, homeowners association dues, insurance, and maintenance eat into your profit. Renting it out does provide an income stream, but managing the property and dealing with tenants is a hassle. Sure, you can hire a property manager, but that has disadvantages of its own, not the least of which is the additional expense.

"I understand all that," you say, "but I'm not looking for a rental property. I just want a nice vacation home now that I'm retired, a place to idle away the hours and visit with my kids and grandkids." An idyllic notion, but this too is better in theory than it is in practice. In my experience working with retirees, the vacation home often becomes more of a burden than a blessing. It can make you feel pinned down, emotionally as well as financially. You feel obligated to spend time there instead of venturing to all the far-flung places you dreamed you'd one day visit when you no longer had to work. And "weekends away" become "weekends at Home Depot buying paint and spackle" because every month something else gets chipped or broken or needs an upgrade. Mutual funds might be unexciting, but you never need to give them a fresh coat of paint.

By all means, take long vacations, and bring along the whole brood, but don't be tied down to one property in one location. With the advent of Airbnb and Vrbo, it's easier than ever to rent a home for weeks at a time, whether it's a little condo for just the two of you or an eight-bedroom mansion for children, grandchildren, siblings, nieces, and nephews. And instead of buying a second house, invest your money where it will more efficiently work for you.

THE EXCEPTION TO THE RULE

Personal finance is all about balancing personal and material goals in the pursuit of what's important to you. And in special cases, the most financially prudent option might not actually be the best one.

I had a pair of clients, a married couple who also happened to live down the street from me, so I knew their family well. They were coasting along toward retirement, but everything changed when the husband developed Alzheimer's at age sixty. Within a year, he lost his job and had to go on disability. This was emotionally and financially devastating to his wife, who had suddenly become the caregiver for an ailing husband whose mind was in rapid decline. It was tragic.

A few years later, as she was walking to the kitchen to bring her husband some tea, she suffered a fatal heart attack and died right there in the living room. By this point the husband's mental faculties had deteriorated so much that he could barely communicate. It's likely he wasn't even quite sure what was going on or knew his dear wife had passed just steps away. Thirty-six hours went by before anyone found her.

Fortunately, she had left clear end-of-life instructions to her daughters, and they knew to call me. We spoke about their options, including what they could do about their widowed dad. One of the daughters opted to move in with her father and to take care of him, even though she had two kids of her own and was going through a divorce at the time.

She ended up having to put him in a facility where he could get the care he needed. She just couldn't do it all by herself. And within a few years, he, too, passed away, leaving his daughters a generous inheritance.

The two daughters responded very differently to this windfall. The one who had been caring for her dad said, "Patrick, just keep the money where it is. I don't need it now. I'll just take the inherited IRA distributions."

The other daughter wanted to buy a beach home. I admit that at first, I judged her decision hastily, especially in light of her sister's frugality and prudence. Was she really going to blow it all on a beach home? It didn't seem like a good move.

When I met with her, I told her why I thought this and explained why from an investment standpoint, it might not work out, but she was adamant about it.

It took me by surprise when she started tearing up in my office.

"I know it's maybe not the wisest purchase," she said. "But it's not about the money. When we were growing up, every summer we used to go to Sunset Beach on the Carolina coast. Me, my sister, Mom, and Dad. And I always dreamed that we would be able to continue that tradition with my kids and my sister's kids. And now that my folks are gone, it's more important to me than ever. That we can still do things together as a family. And Mom and Dad will still be there with us, in a way."

It was a reminder that it's not always about the numbers. You have to weigh the return on investment against the emotional benefit that is derived. Financially, it wasn't the best choice, but to her, it meant so much more than that. It was about keeping her parents' memories alive and staying close with her sister and her nieces. Some things truly matter more than money.

ILLIQUID OR NONPUBLICLY TRADED REAL ESTATE INVESTMENT TRUSTS

Bill is one of those guys who acts completely different over email than in real life. When we correspond to set up meetings, his terse, borderline abrasive tone makes me start bracing myself for a difficult client meeting. But then when he walks through the door, he's happy as a clam, eager to dispense with a joke and receive one in kind. An all-around good guy to work with.

Bill is retired, but he's still trying to unravel some bad decisions from his previous broker, who sold him a bunch of nonpublicly traded real estate investment trusts (REITs). Because they're not publicly traded, they're highly illiquid, nor are they subject to the same transparency rules as public REITs, which they significantly underperform. The reason brokers like to push this kind of investment is—you guessed it—high fees and commissions, usually 6 to 12 percent, which go right into the broker's pocket.

Bill needed help to find a way to unload his REIT shares in a cost-effective manner. We figured out a plan, but the most he could redeem was 5 percent of his holdings each quarter. At that rate, it'll take twenty quarters (five years) to get his money out of this REIT that he probably never should have invested in in the first place.

Don't make the same mistake. Some real estate exposure is good, but nontraded REITs are not the way to do it.

THE MARKET IS YOUR FRIEND

Nobody can predict the future. But you don't need to, to be successful.

Savvy investing doesn't depend on tricks, gimmicks, insider knowledge, or crystal ball clairvoyance. It doesn't require an advanced math degree, sophisticated technical analysis, guru-like knowledge of the market, or Vegas-style risk taking. All it requires is a simple and straightforward approach based on putting capital into proven diversified investments, while minimizing trading and maximizing patience. This approach is unflashy and unsexy and doesn't impress anyone at parties, but it *will* generate the kind of gains that reliably build wealth over the long term. The market is your friend. Don't try to outwit it. Just go along with it; let the market work for you, doing what it does best: taking the capital invested in it to produce more capital.

The market is your friend. Don't try to outwit it.

TAKEAWAYS:

1. Historically, stocks outperform bonds, value stocks exceed growth stocks, small companies do better than large ones, and profitable firms beat out less profitable ones. There are many exceptions to these rules, and year-to-year performance fluctuates wildly, but decade to decade, these guidelines are proven moneymakers.

2. If you have enough capital to purchase a second home, whether as a vacation getaway or a rental property, other investments (such as mutual funds) are probably a better option. A second house is rarely worth the headache and expense.

3. Don't try to time the market. It's almost impossible to do, even for the experts. "Buy and hold" is not only easier; the returns will be better over a long time frame.

CHAPTER FIVE

THE PORTFOLIO PAYCHECK

I f you've been drawing a steady paycheck for nearly half a century, retirement can feel like having the financial rug pulled out from under you, regardless of how much you've saved. Receiving a "portfolio paycheck" eases the psychological effect of no longer drawing a salary, encourages financial discipline by helping you stick to a budget, and provides regular cash infusions to pay for expenses and enjoy your postemployment life.

For someone on the cusp of retirement, many important questions loom: "How much do I need each month to maintain my lifestyle? What assets do I need to sell to fund that lifestyle? Which accounts do I draw from? And how often?" It can be daunting, especially when you pile on all the other life changes brought about by retirement.

Spending money that you've spent your whole life accumulating and having to make it last until death (or beyond, if you intend to bequeath something to your loved ones) can be unnerving. People often say they don't want to touch the principal; they want to live off only interest or dividends. But that's rarely practical—at some point you're going to have to dip into the principal, particularly as values fluctuate or we face a recession.

Nevertheless, a well-constructed portfolio should provide the funds you need when you need them, putting you in an optimal position to sell shares periodically while still maintaining your wealth. If you're adequately diversified, you'll be able to sell something that's performed well rather than being forced to liquidate an asset at an inopportune time. In that sense, setting up the portfolio paycheck begins long before retirement. You have to lay the groundwork in your forties, fifties, and sixties for a comfortable life in the decades that follow.

HOW IT WORKS

As an example, let's imagine somebody who is sixty-six years old with a $3 million portfolio. Their total monthly living expenses, including healthcare costs, are $10,000. They'll get $2,500 a month from Social Security, which they'll start receiving when they officially retire next month. That leaves $7,500 monthly ($90,000 a year) that we have to transfer from their existing accounts to cover their expenses.

Managing the portfolio paycheck is largely a matter of balancing risk (market exposure) and reward (cash preservation). With that in mind, we run a few calculations to determine the highest risk that this person could tolerate. Since we plan for a ten-year cash need basis, we need to account for $900,000 for the next decade. To play it safe, we take that $900,000 (30 percent of total assets) and move it to some type of capital preservation portfolio heavy on bonds and cash, things that won't lose a lot of value in a down market.

We try to keep about three to six months' worth of cash in their portfolio at all times, probably in a higher yielding money market mutual fund to maximize the interest. Then every month we'll automatically transfer $7,500 into their checking account.

Now eventually, if they've put aside only three to six months in cash, they're going to have to start pulling from the portfolio to raise funds for the next three to six months. That's when we turn to the other side of the portfolio, the remaining 70 percent that has more exposure to the market. If the market is healthy and stocks are doing well, it might be time to sell to come up with the next three to six months of cash ($45,000).

If the market is slumping (as it did in 2020), the client won't necessarily be forced to sell stocks because 30 percent of their portfolio is already safeguarded in capital preservation. You can't control what the market does, but you can always control what you do. And careful planning, proper diversification, and adhering to a chosen risk ratio (70/30 in this case) allows you to remain in control—to have options and to choose prudently rather than out of desperation. Even if the market is plummeting, don't let it force your hand.

I think where a lot of advisors and investors err is when they say, "Hey, I don't want to sell something if it's performing really well." But actually, that's when you're supposed to be pulling some of the chips off the table and do some rebalancing. Conversely, if an asset has declined, rather than sell, you should normally rebalance by buying more of it at a better price.

Naturally, we make adjustments as time goes by, either to account for higher income (you start collecting Social Security or a pension) or higher expenses. Healthcare costs tend to rise as people get up in years, so we factor in such changes as they happen. A million different things can happen that shift the ten-year cash need target.

Some people opt for a more conservative risk ratio, especially if their living expenses aren't as high and their tolerance for volatility is low. They might go with a 50/50 mix for the rest of their life because they can safely draw from the cash preservation side without having to worry too much about portfolio growth. You still have to do the ten-year cash need analysis, but in this case, it's not as much of a moving target.

WHAT IF I RUN OUT OF MONEY?

This is obviously a retiree's worst nightmare: your account statements are flirting with zero at an age when you can't really go back to work and no one will extend you credit. Living on Social Security alone is a bleak prospect. However, for people of a reasonably high net worth, it's highly unlikely, as long as you stick to the plan.

> Living on Social Security alone is a bleak prospect. However, for people of a reasonably high net worth, it's highly unlikely, as long as you stick to the plan.

It's true that some people do blow through heaps of cash in their elderly years, but as an advisor, I usually see the warning signs on the horizon. If I sense that a client's lifestyle is imperiling their financial longevity, then I'll candidly tell them that their current spending habits are not sustainable. If they refuse to listen to my advice, then we're probably not going to continue to work together.

During a long bull market, running out of money understandably becomes less of a concern since your portfolio is still growing in value. I was just talking to a seventy-eight-year-old client down in Florida who has been pulling out his required minimum distributions from his IRA for the last eight years but is baffled by the fact that he has more money now than when he started! That's due to the epic, record-setting bull run that began in 2009.

Retirees really start fretting during an economic slowdown. When I got into the business in 1998, the tech bubble was at its peak, and irrational exuberance had investors of all stripes pouring their capital into a meteoric market. A few years later, the bubble burst, a recession clobbered the economy, and 9/11 happened. The same people who were buoyed into retirement (sometimes an early one) by the tech boom suddenly panicked when they saw their holdings crater. Some younger retirees had to go back to work. Older ones had to find a way to manage. It was tough.

Of course, this is why you hire an advisor: anyone can build wealth when the bulls are in charge, but a skilled advisor can guide you through the difficult periods, even when you're no longer employed. I've never had any retired clients run out of money because we design a system and stick with it, fine-tuning it as needed. Just keep your expenses in check, remain properly insured to prevent a healthcare disaster, stay disciplined in your investments, and avoid taking on massive debt, and you should be okay.

PAYING DOWN YOUR MORTGAGE (AND OTHER DEBT)

For the retiree living off a portfolio paycheck, eliminating that monthly mortgage payment is the equivalent of a huge salary boost. And it gives you a tremendous sense of levity when a debt you've carried for decades is finally paid off.

In times when the market is up (with annual returns between 8 and 10 percent) and interest rates are down (hovering around 3 percent), wouldn't you be better off putting that money in stocks? It's a fair question, and you can make the case for postponing paying off your house in favor of investing more in the market. Some advisors differentiate between "good debt" (like a mortgage) and "bad debt" (like credit cards) and reason that in a strong economy, it's preferable to keep that money in my portfolio instead of paying down low-interest-deductible debt.

However, I'm more debt averse, and I think the psychological benefit from clearing your mortgage in retirement is reason enough to do it. It's also worth mentioning that for advisors who are paid a percentage of assets under management, there's a certain conflict of interest in encouraging people to keep that money in their portfolio. Beyond that, one must also consider the ever-present possibility that 10 percent annual gains go flat or turn negative, thus changing the equation.

Basically, it comes down to your individual personality and needs. I do often recommend that clients, during their working years, get a home equity line of credit to access the equity in their home if needed. It's harder for retirees to qualify for a home equity loan since their income has stopped. Also, many retirees are now taking the standard deduction rather than itemizing mortgage interest, so in their case any tax benefits of having a mortgage on their primary residence are nullified. In any case, in my experience, nobody has ever expressed regret for paying off their house early.

I'm working with a couple now for whom the psychological boost of being debt free has been a powerful incentive. The husband and wife are forty-three years old and have three kids. Epilepsy has rendered the husband, a physician, unable to work. Fortunately, he has good disability insurance that puts $14,000 in his account each month, tax free, until age sixty-eight, and his wife is still gainfully employed.

So they're managing financially, but emotionally, it's a lot to bear, especially at such a young age and when faced with the prospect of multiple brain surgeries, long recovery periods, lifetime drug regimens, and other medical and physical challenges. They've told me that given their current predicament, their priority now is just to get the house paid off. It will give them some much-needed peace of mind. If the husband were to die prematurely and the disability income stops, the wife wants to know she's not going to have to worry about having to make the mortgage payment to prevent the bank foreclosing on their house and her having to uproot their kids. I agree it's the right move for them. This worked out particularly well because they were able to pay off the mortgage before the COVID-19 pandemic and subsequent 30 percent-plus downturn in global stock prices. While we never try to "time" the market, this worked out wonderfully.

Besides a mortgage, other forms of debt also afflict people later in life. It's not uncommon for high-net-worth individuals to still be paying off student loans long after earning their degrees. You can guess who I'm talking about—doctors, orthodontists, and lawyers whose education ran them a quarter of a million dollars or more.

Some people wonder how attorneys and physicians could still be carrying massive debt despite earning well into the six figures annually. Well, as I've come to learn in my practice, the guy writing your prescriptions or peering into your mouth to check out your incisors might not be as fiscally responsible as you'd think. I've seen it often: doctors who grind ten years out in school finally start making bank, and they go a little nuts: buying a boat here, a beach house there, living the high life while putting debt repayment on hold. Some of them understand that when they die, their education loans die with them, particularly if the loan is unsecured, which means that it's forgiven when the debtor passes away.

In that case, the loan won't follow you to the pearly gates (though given the persistence of some lenders, I wouldn't be surprised if they tried, Saint Peter's do-not-call list notwithstanding), but it's still a psychological weight hanging over you. If you're pulling in half a mil annually, isn't it worth it to just get rid of it? If it were me, I'd rather be free and in the clear.

YOUR NEW "CAREER"

Some people are under the impression that when they retire, their finances get much simpler and easier, but there's still a lot of work to do even after you stop working. Wealth accumulation (working and saving) is the easy part. You're just socking money away and forgetting about it.

The distribution phase is more challenging. When you retire, you have to figure out how to effectively pull money out of your accounts, manage taxes, and stay within your budget. You have to be more precise and systematic and stick to a plan, not just for ten years but in all likelihood twenty or thirty years at least.

And that's why I think a lot of salesmen out there try to sling annuities at people. They're selling the convenience of a guaranteed payment for the rest of your life so "you don't even have to worry about it." And some people cling to that security blanket. But if you believe in the markets throughout your investing career, you should be able to withdraw steadily from your own portfolio without having to worry about running out, even with inflation and a progressive rise in expenses as you get older.

Retirement is not just a brief "waiting room to heaven" or "a few pickleball tournaments until you die." Thirty-year retirements have become the norm. And if you're going to spend a good part of your lifetime in retirement, you better figure out a way to manage your money well to balance the need for growth along with the need for capital preservation.

> If you believe in the markets throughout your investing career, you should be able to withdraw steadily from your own portfolio without having to worry about running out, even with inflation and a progressive rise in expenses as you get older.

You're no longer working, but you do have a new career: enjoying retirement. Shouldn't you get regularly paid for it?

TAKEAWAYS:

1. "How much money should I save for retirement?" is perhaps the biggest question on everyone's mind. And the obvious answer is "everyone is different." But most of our clients have a high probability of achieving their goals and not running out of money at $2 million. According to the *New York Times*, for people sixty-five and older, a net worth of $2 million puts you in the top 10 percent. One million dollars places you roughly in the top 20 percent.[14] So a couple mil is a good target.

2. Your cash need influences how aggressive or conservative you'll want to be in retirement. Like everything else, it requires the right balance. For most people, 70/30 is a good mix; others with lower expenses and a lower tolerance for risk can manage with a 50/50 ratio.

3. Pay off debt! You've worked too hard and too long to have any kind of debt, good or bad, hanging over your head. The benefits of doing so are emotional as well as financial.

---

14   "Are you rich? Where does your net worth rank in America?" *New York Times,* Aug. 12, 2019, https://www.nytimes.com/interactive/2019/08/12/upshot/are-you-rich-where-does-your-net-worth-rank-wealth.html.

CHAPTER SIX

HOW TAX EFFICIENCIES CAN BENEFIT YOU

Nothing is certain in life but death, taxes, and someone quoting Ben Franklin whenever this subject comes up. As an advisor, when it comes to taxation, my goal is simply for the client to pay the least amount of tax legally allowed. This chapter will give you some pointers on how to do just that.

It may surprise you to hear that many advisors don't give much thought to their clients' taxes, to the clients' own detriment. Recently I took on a new client who came to me stark raving mad about his former advisor, with whom his professional relationship was rather short lived. The reason it was short lived was because when Sam signed up, the new advisor instructed Sam to liquidate his whole portfolio and buy various bonds, stocks, and exchange-traded funds to conform to the advisor's usual approach to client investment. But these sales triggered over a million dollars in capital gains taxes.

Sam went ballistic and demanded to know why his advisor hadn't warned him about the tax consequences, but the advisor deflected any and all blame and just said, "Well, talk to your CPA. Taxes are his job!"

> Any half-decent advisor will factor taxes into a client's financial calculus.

No. They're our job too. Any half-decent advisor will factor taxes into a client's financial calculus. There are a lot of moving parts with tax, and you have to look at everything with a 360-degree, four-dimensional view to reduce the effect. One wrong move can touch off a cascade of adverse effects. Fortunately, there are a number of little things that can save tax dollars over time.

POSITIONING ASSETS TO CREATE A TAX-EFFICIENT PORTFOLIO: ASSET LOCATION

Asset location concerns the location of assets in a taxable or a tax-advantaged account. Prudent asset location helps investors defer or eliminate taxes. It makes a *big* difference over a long timeline.

The general rule of thumb is that you want to have your less tax-efficient investments, like government and corporate bonds as well as REITs that generate a lot of interest and dividends, held in tax-deferred accounts such as IRAs or 401(k)s so they can grow without having to pay taxes up front. More tax-efficient investments like stocks and tax-free municipal bonds should be in taxable accounts, such as nonqualified, non-IRA, or brokerage accounts.

One of my clients is a fifty-three-year-old who wants to pay down his mortgage, which of course is something I generally encourage, but I've counseled him to funnel his money into his 401(k) instead. He's in his peak earning years, and he and his wife are pulling down $300,000 annually, but he's investing only $9,000 each year into his 401(k), which you can max out at $19,500 (plus $6,500 more in catch-up if you're over fifty). That's all pretax income that comes straight off the top.

A married couple with income of $300,000 is in the 24 percent marginal tax bracket for federal taxes. You can add 5.25 percent North Carolina state tax on top of that. If they put $26,000 into a 401(k), this couple's taxable income becomes $274,000 instead of $300,000, effectively saving them 29.25 cents of every dollar between $274,000 and $300,000. They'll have to pay tax at some point when they make withdrawals from the 401(k), but probably at a lower rate when they are in retirement because by that point they won't have so much earned income from work. 401(k) contributions directly reduce adjusted gross income (AGI) and modified adjusted gross income (MAGI), both of which are the key determinants for phaseouts of various tax rules.

Put simply, when it comes to 401(k)s, max out your contributions! They offer the biggest bang for your buck since they're tax deferred—you don't pay taxes until you withdraw, provided you wait until age 59½. (Before that, there's a 10 percent early withdrawal penalty). It's one of the best tax savings vehicles out there.

Another very general guideline is to have more of your fixed income exposure in a traditional IRA and more of your stock exposure in a brokerage account. Roth IRAs are a good place to stack up on aggressive investments because those dollars are all growing tax free. Global real estate, emerging markets, small-cap stocks—asset classes that have the greatest probability of achieving higher returns over time. Since the Roth IRA grows tax free (not just tax deferred), it's an optimal vehicle for securities with more upside potential and generous dividends. The compound interest effect of securities with higher return potential in a tax-free vehicle is very powerful.

Moreover, unless it's inherited, you also don't have to take required minimum distributions (RMDs) from Roth IRAs, which means this vehicle can grow tax free for a long, long time! Your beneficiaries will enjoy inheriting Roth IRAs because they get to withdraw the money tax free as well.

Other great things about a Roth IRA: (1) it's not considered income in the provisional income calculation that determines taxability of Social Security benefits, (2) it's not included in AGI, and (3) it's not included in the calculation for Medicare surcharges.

"I MAKE TOO MUCH TO MAKE IRA CONTRIBUTIONS"

There are income limits to taking a *deduction* for contributions to a traditional IRA. However, anybody, regardless of income, can still *make* a contribution. It's still great to get tax-deferred growth in an account, even if it's not tax deductible.

Roth IRAs have income eligibility rules: if you're a single person who makes more than $139,000 or a married couple earning $206,000 (as of 2020), you can't contribute. However, if you're ineligible for a Roth IRA, consider the little-known backdoor Roth IRA, a loophole that allows high income earners to contribute to a Roth IRA anyway.

It works like this: you make a nondeductible contribution to a traditional IRA (without claiming a tax deduction for the contribution). Then transfer the funds to a Roth IRA through a "conversion."

This is something my wife and I use for ourselves. Normally, we'd be ineligible for Roth IRA contributions because our combined income is too high. But regardless of how much money I make, I can contribute to a traditional IRA for her, and I can immediately turn around and convert that to a Roth IRA. And because it hasn't grown at all, there are no tax consequences or penalties.

Normally, if you were to convert a traditional IRA to a Roth IRA, you would have to pay taxes because you've made a deduction for putting that money in; you haven't paid any tax on it yet. In this case, I'm making an *after*-tax contribution through a traditional IRA, and now that Roth IRA money is going to grow tax free for the rest of her life until she starts taking distributions. The good thing about Roth IRAs is not only do they grow tax free, but there's no RMD that she'll have to take at age seventy-two. It's another easy way to add tax-free growth to your portfolio and diversify your income stream in retirement.

MANAGING YOUR RMDS

When you hit 72 (previously 70½, but the SECURE Act changed that as of 2020), the IRS is going to require you to start withdrawing from traditional IRAs and rollover IRAs whether you need the money or not. (Another change brought about by the new law: "stretch IRAs" are no longer allowed—inherited IRAs must be distributed within ten years).

Most people end up accumulating the bulk of their wealth in 401(k)s and IRAs, and if you're holding a few million, the RMD can reach into the hundreds of thousands of dollars. "I have too much money on hand!" is perhaps one of the better positions in life to be in, but the problem is that if the distributions are high, it inadvertently forces people into higher income tax brackets, which means higher taxes and higher Medicare premiums.

There are some things you can do to mitigate this. Let's say a married couple has $1 million in 401(k)s and IRAs and $200,000 in a brokerage account. They're both sixty-seven years old, recently retired, and currently have taxable income of $50,000 between Social Security, a small pension, and some interest and dividends. The 12 percent federal marginal tax bracket ends at $80,250; for incomes of $80,251 to $171,050, the marginal rate almost doubles to 22 percent. If they had to take an RMD from their $1 million IRA or 401(k) today, it would mean roughly an extra $37,000 in taxable income, thus raising their income to at least $87,000 instead of $50,000 and pushing them into the 22 percent marginal bracket.

Since they have a couple of years until age seventy-two, why not convert approximately $30,000 of their IRA into a Roth IRA to bring their total taxable income closer to the upper limit of the 12 percent federal marginal bracket of $80,250, instead of keeping their income at $50,000? They would pay 12 percent federal marginal tax on this money now as a result of the conversion instead of paying 22 percent in five years when they are over seventy-two.

This way, not only will they pay a lower rate now, but it also reduces the IRA and 401(k) balance that will be subject to RMDs once they reach seventy-two.

In addition, if they are receiving Social Security, there is a calculation of their provisional income that determines how much of their Social Security payment is taxable. If we executed the Roth conversion strategy, the couple might have to pay tax on their Social Security payments.

Therefore, be aware that a Roth conversion to this income threshold could trigger more taxes due on Social Security income received. It's a balancing act.

Another stratagem would be to just delay taking their Social Security and withdraw the assets from their IRAs to meet their income needs. Social Security credits your future payments 8 percent each year you delay from full retirement age until seventy. Therefore, they can pay 12 percent federal tax on the IRA distributions and earn a guaranteed 8 percent rate on their Social Security payment.

We can do Roth conversions (moving money from a traditional IRA into a Roth IRA) over five to ten years, depending on the age of retirement. For example, if a couple retired at sixty-two, they could do these smaller Roth conversions for the next ten years. The more money we can convert to a Roth IRA, the better, since we get tax-free compound interest in the Roth IRA while reducing RMDs from the traditional IRA.

In an effort to help Americans during the COVID-19 pandemic, the CARES Act legislation suspended RMDs for 2020. This is a tremendous tax savings for many retired investors who have other income sources from which to draw a portfolio paycheck. In addition, it also provides another opportunity to execute Roth conversions for both retired investors and those still working. For example, a retired investor over the age of seventy-two, who might normally be required to distribute $50,000 as an RMD, could instead use 2020 as an opportunity to convert that same $50,000 to a Roth IRA. The tax liability would be the same, but now the money is put in a Roth IRA for tax-free growth going forward. In addition, because IRA values are 20 to 30 percent lower than the highs they may have reached in February 2020, an investor is able to convert more shares at a lower price.

SOCIAL SECURITY: MYTHS AND REALITIES

Retirees are often surprised to learn that the tax man will come for their Social Security income too. If a married couple's provisional income—gross income plus tax-free interest plus 50 percent of Social Security benefits—exceeds $44,000, up to 85 percent of that is subject to tax (though of course that doesn't mean that the tax *rate* is 85 percent).

This is where retirement income distribution becomes more art than science, because the usual approach is to take from your brokerage accounts and tax and savings first while letting the IRAs continue to grow tax deferred for as long as possible, especially Roth IRAs that are growing tax free. However, for some people, it's actually the opposite: it's better from a tax standpoint to start taking money from their Roth IRA first because that's not included in the provisional income calculation for the taxability of Social Security. It really just depends on the financial profile of the individual.

> Taking money from a Roth IRA or from a brokerage account first sometimes makes a lot more sense because it keeps Social Security taxes low and Medicare premiums lower.

Other factors are at play too. A Roth IRA is a great asset to be able to pass down to children and grandchildren because they won't have to pay tax on it either, but if you don't have any beneficiaries, your primary concern is the amount of tax that you're going to pay during your own life. Therefore, taking money from a Roth IRA or from a brokerage account first sometimes makes a lot more sense because it keeps Social Security taxes low and Medicare premiums lower.

MEDICARE PREMIUM SURCHARGE

One big area of concern is the Medicare premium surcharge. A lot of people don't realize that once your MAGI exceeds $174,000 for a married couple, you end up paying much more for your Medicare Part B and Part D premiums. Recently, I had to temper the enthusiasm of a client who was telling me how he can't wait to get on Medicare because "I'll finally save some money on healthcare!" Maybe he'll pay less than he does now for private insurance, but because his income is so high, he's actually going to be paying about $500 a month for his Medicare for Part B and Part D, versus $144.60 a month for a married couple making under $174,000. Five hundred dollars versus $144.60 every month per spouse really adds up.

For people over 70½, qualified charitable distributions (which we'll discuss more in chapter 8) can directly help reduce their MAGI for Medicare purposes. In addition, executing some Roth IRA conversions before age seventy-two can also reduce the MAGI for future years.

The years before RMDs start are an opportune time to convert a portion of IRA dollars into a Roth IRA so that, because they are in a Roth, they won't be subject to RMDs once the investor hits age seventy-two.

If the investor is not retired yet, but over sixty-five and receiving Medicare, they could also max out 401(k) contributions to knock off a few more dollars from their taxable income.

Finally, health savings account distributions for qualified medical expenses when someone is on Medicare are tax free; thus, they don't affect your MAGI for Medicare premium purposes.

HEALTH SAVINGS ACCOUNTS

Let's talk a little more about health savings accounts (HSAs), an oft-overlooked, poorly understood benefit of the tax code. HSAs let individuals and families enrolled in *tax-qualified high-deductible plans* sock away money for future healthcare expenses. Besides its primary use as a medical rainy day fund, it's another way of reducing your taxable income. Families are able to put $7,100 away annually, and if you're over fifty-five, you can top it off with an extra $1,000 dollars. If you use it for medical costs, it's never taxed. Moreover, a number of HSAs now offer investment opportunities, so not only is there a tax advantage but the money can also grow while it sits there.

If you set aside $8,100 each year for ten years, never touching it and letting its value appreciate, you could have a $100,000 account available just for healthcare needs that will inevitably happen in retirement.

After age sixty-five, if you still have money in it, there's no penalty for withdrawals, even if you don't use the funds for health expenses. Use all that tax-free money as you see fit. It essentially becomes a de facto second Roth IRA for you, but you enjoyed a tax deduction going in. So in that sense it's even better than a Roth IRA.

Note that I said it must be a *high deductible* health plan. With insurance, there's generally a trade-off between premiums and deductibles: a higher deductible/lower premium plan is preferable for someone who doesn't expect to see the doctor a lot. Conversely, a lower deductible/higher premium plan is probably more cost effective for someone with a lot of medical needs.

In practice, the problem with HSAs is that with high deductible health plans, the premiums are generally not much cheaper than a regular deductible health plan. So you're risking the high deductible should you ever need to see the doctor but still paying a premium that is only negligibly lower (when making an apples-to-apples comparison—i.e., a gold plan PPO versus a gold plan HSA).

Nevertheless, we encourage the use of HSAs, which are puzzlingly underused by the general public (perhaps because people just don't understand them). Healthcare can be expensive even for the well insured, and it's nice to have some savings stored away for that purpose. If you never use it, well, then you have a nice "mini-Roth IRA" for which to do what you wish when you turn sixty-five.

529 EDUCATION SAVINGS ACCOUNTS

Created in 1996, 529 plans are state-sponsored savings vehicles operated by a state or educational institution designed to help families save for future college costs. While they used to only be applicable for higher education expenses, in 2018, these savings vehicles were expanded to include K–12 education—up to $10,000 of tuition per year, per child. I think that can be helpful for a grandparent who wants to help their grandchild pay for private school. Some states also allow you a state income tax deduction if you contribute to a 529 plan.

In addition, the SECURE Act now allows families to take tax-free 529 plan distributions for student loan repayment. The law includes an aggregate lifetime limit of $10,000 in qualified student loan repayments per 529 plan beneficiary. The SECURE Act also allows 529 Plans to be used to pay for apprenticeship programs.

There are two types of plans: savings plans, which allow you to contribute dollars and choose from several different investment options, and prepaid plans, which allow you to prepay all or part of the costs of an in-state public college education. The independent 529 plan is also available to prepay tuition at private and independent colleges. We'll focus on savings plans for now.

Advantages of 529 savings plans include the following:

- Tax deferral (no federal tax deduction on contributions)

- Potential federal tax-free distributions if used for qualified higher education expenses

- Potential state tax deduction (if home state plan is used, and home state allows state tax deductions)

- Owner retains control of assets, and there is no date by which funds must be used

- Ability to make substantial deposits, up to $300,000 in some states

- Contributions are completed gifts and removed from the contributor's estate—which can be an effective estate planning tool

- Ability to change beneficiaries

- No restrictions on choice of college, as long as it's accredited

- Anyone can contribute on behalf of a beneficiary, and low minimum investments to initiate

Like HSAs, 529 plans can be invested in mutual funds, which offer better returns than a simple interest-generating savings account but of course also involve more risk if the market tanks. And withdrawals are penalized at 10 percent if they're not used for qualified educational expenses.

LESSER-KNOWN TAX-SAVING TRICKS

These methods are a bit technical, but they can save you some extra dollars.

THE MUTUAL FUND TAX TRAP

Mutual funds are required to distribute dividends and capital gains each year. While not a major concern in tax-deferred accounts like 401(k)s and IRAs, these can create unexpected taxes in nonqualified accounts. Pay close attention to the mutual fund's expected distribution date and the amount of distribution.

Here are some issues to consider for nonqualified accounts:

- If it's near the end of a calendar year, you may want to wait to purchase in a nonqualified account until after distributions are made to avoid taxation on a recent acquisition. Distributions are generally made toward the end of the year (November and December). Mutual fund companies typically release the expected distribution amount in advance to prepare taxpayers.

- If you are considering selling a mutual fund in a nonqualified account and the fund is expected to distribute a significant amount of capital gains and dividends, you might want to sell the fund before distributions. That said, taxes should not be the only factor in your decision.

EXAMPLE

December 15: Julie purchases $25,000 of ABC Mutual Fund at $10.00 a share	2,500 shares at $10.00 each
December 22: ABC Mutual Fund distributes $0.50 long-term capital gain per share	$0.50 LTCG per share
Those gains are reinvested in the fund	Reinvestments of gains
Julie now owns	2631.58 shares with a market value of $9.50 per share: $25,000
Julie has a long-term capital gain tax liability	2,500 shares x $0.50 gain per share = $1,250

NET UNREALIZED APPRECIATION

Net Unrealized Appreciation (NUA) is the difference in value between the average cost basis of company shares held in a qualified company plan and the current market value of the shares. A potential tax-savings strategy exists for individuals who maintain highly appreciated employer stock within a qualified plan like a 401(k).

Step 1: Instead of performing a direct rollover of the appreciated stock, you may consider transferring the company stock to a regular (nonqualified) brokerage account. The investor will then owe ordinary income tax on the cost basis of the transferred stock, not the current market value.

Step 2: If the company stock is then sold after distribution, the investor will pay long-term capital gains tax on the NUA. If the investor decides to hold the stock after distribution, any additional gain over the NUA will be taxed at either long- or short-term capital gains tax rates, depending on how long the shares are held after distribution.

For example, John is an employee of XYZ Company and has a 401(k) worth $500,000. Three hundred thousand of his 401(k) is in XYZ Company stock with an average cost basis of $50,000. The remaining $200,000 in John's 401(k) is invested in various mutual funds within the 401(k) plan.

John executes the NUA strategy upon separation from the company. His shares in XYZ stock are transferred to a nonqualified brokerage account as a taxable distribution based on his average cost basis. The remaining $200,000 in mutual fund assets is directly rolled over into an IRA.

Tax Consequences at Distribution	IRS Treatment	When Taxes Will Be Due
$50,000 (XYZ cost basis)	Ordinary Income	At distribution
$250,000 (appreciation)	Long-term capital gains	If sold when received (assuming XYZ stock has not appreciated further)
Change in value after distribution from XYZ plan	Long- or short-term capital gain/loss based on change in value of XYZ stock*	Based on tax year in which XYZ stock is sold

* Depending on the length of time the stock is held after distribution
Example is hypothetical and for educational purposes only.

2018 TAX LAW: WHAT YOU SHOULD KNOW

Tax law has never been simple, but the passage of the 2018 federal tax reform introduced a whole new set of complexities into determining who owes what. Bad news for taxpayers; good news, I suppose, for accountants, tax attorneys, and financial advisors everywhere, who have probably enjoyed some extra business as people look to maximize their options and take advantage of new loopholes, deductions, and exemptions.

We won't delve into all the nuances of the law, but there are a few key changes you should be aware of.

At TFA, the biggest effect on our clients was the increase in the standard deduction: for single people, it's $12,400, and for a married couple, it's $24,800. For most of our retirees, if they have their houses paid off and are no longer taking the mortgage interest deduction, they just opt for the standard deduction over itemized deductions.

Another big change is the state and local income tax cap; now, you can deduct a max of $10,000. In states with high income taxes like New Jersey and New York, it's not uncommon to see people paying $10,000-plus just for property taxes. In North Carolina, where I live, if you're making $200,000 a year, you pay 5.25 percent tax—that's $10,500 a year you're paying in state income taxes. Then let's say you paid another $11,000 a year in property taxes—before, you could deduct that $21,500. Now, it's capped at $10,000. That has certainly had an effect on people who pay a lot in property taxes or state income taxes.

Another notable change was increasing the estate tax exemption per spouse from $5.49 million in 2017 to $11.58 million in 2020. This affects few people, but for the select few with massive estates (or, more precisely, for their heirs), it's a huge windfall. Technically, a married couple could leave $23.16 million to beneficiaries without it being subject to estate tax. When I started in the business in '98, the estate tax exemption was $625,000. To think it's gone up by a factor of eighteen over the past twenty years is insane.

The 2018 law also lowered the mortgage interest tax deduction from $1 million to $750,000, but more people have been affected by using a home equity line of credit. The interest used to be deductible regardless of what you used the money for. You could buy a car or pay off debt, and the interest would be deductible. The new rule says it's only deductible if you use the funds to buy, build, or substantially improve the home that's securing the debt, and this amount is rolled into the $750,000 cap of the home acquisition debt.

Additionally, the child and dependent tax credit was increased to $2,000 per child, of which $1,400 is refundable. The new law also created a $500 nonrefundable credit for qualifying dependents other than children. A bigger improvement for many was increasing the income threshold phaseout to $400,000 for those married filing jointly, when it used to be $110,000.

Finally, the law introduced a bevy of changes for corporations and business owners, though taking advantage of these changes is pretty tricky. If you're a business owner with pass-through income, you may be able to deduct up to 20 percent of your business income. This is known as the QBI deduction. A lot of businesses (like mine) were excluded from this: law firms, medical practices, consulting firms, professional athletes, accountants, financial advisors, performers, and investment managers. Businesses involved in real estate, however, can avail themselves of the deduction.

TAXES: IT'S ACCRUAL WORLD

In truth, it's a challenge to write about how to optimize (i.e., minimize) your taxes. That's because everyone's tax situation is unique, and there are few general-izations you can make about what's best for all parties. Neverthe-less, finding legal tax loopholes and shelters and understanding that

> Finding legal tax loopholes and shelters and understanding that taxation is a dynamic part of personal finance that interacts with the other elements are essential to softening the tax bite before and during retirement.

taxation is a dynamic part of personal finance that interacts with the other elements (investment, savings, debt, and charitable giving, which we'll discuss in chapter 8) are essential to softening the tax bite before and during retirement.

TAKEAWAYS:

1. Asset location saves you big money over the long term, especially if you're a top earner. Concentrate tax-inefficient investments (government and corporate bonds, REITS) in tax-deferred accounts such as IRAs or 401(k)s. Tax-efficient investments (stocks, tax-free municipal bonds) should be in taxable accounts, like nonqualified, non-IRA, or brokerage accounts.

2. If you do only one thing to create a tax-efficient portfolio, max out your 401(k). In 2020, that's $19,500 annually that you can contribute, plus $6,500 catch-up for those over fifty years old. Keep in mind this is what employees can contribute—your employer can always contribute additional dollars on your behalf.

3. HSAs and 529 plans are underused but efficient investment vehicles for healthcare and education. And with the HSA, if you haven't spent the money when you turn sixty-five, it's available for you for any purpose, penalty free. Consider it a second Roth IRA.

CHAPTER SEVEN

THE JOYS OF AGING: HEALTHCARE AND OTHER INSURANCE

R ising healthcare costs coupled with inadequate healthcare coverage can have a devastating effect on your retirement plan. A study by Fidelity Investments found that a sixty-five-year-old couple retiring in 2019 will need $285,000 to cover medical expenses throughout retirement.[15] If your goal is to retire early, you

---

15 Meejin Annan-Brady and Michelle Tessier, "Healthcare Price Check," Fidelity Investments, April 2, 2019, https://www.fidelity.com/bin-public/060_www_fidelity_com/documents/press-release/healthcare-price-check-040219.pdf. This figure assumes individuals do not have employer-provided retiree healthcare coverage but do qualify for Medicare.

should have a plan that bridges your healthcare coverage until you become eligible for Medicare at age sixty-five.

If your spouse is still employed and you can get on his or her company health plan, then you're taken care of. Otherwise, navigating the private healthcare market, even with Obamacare and the subsidized marketplace exchanges, is a labyrinthine task that will hit you hard in the pocketbook. It's not uncommon for people in their sixties to pay $2,000 a month for basic health insurance as they wait for Medicare to kick in.

The good news is that once you're finally enrolled in Medicare, it can be a tremendous financial relief. Medicare Part A (hospital insurance) is free. Part B (medical insurance) is around $144.60 a month (though high earners pay more), and the cost of the prescription drug plan (Part D) is pretty nominal. So just reaching your sixty-fifth birthday is usually the biggest healthcare hurdle for older people. However, bear in mind that any healthcare procedure that Medicare deems to be elective will not be covered by Medicare or by your supplemental policy.

Also, Medicare is means tested, so the more income you earn in retirement, the more you're going to pay. For a married couple with a MAGI of more than $174,000, their Medicare premium increases, and for couples with a combined income of between $272,000 and $326,000, the cost is around $376 per month, along with a $50 surcharge per month each for Part D.

As we saw in chapter 6, there are ways of reducing your taxable income, but if your IRA or 401(k) is flush with cash, the RMDs that kick in at seventy-two will likely boost you into a higher income bracket anyway.

Our Medicare specialist refers to Medicare as a "home run" for the vast majority of Americans. This is another thing that makes TFA unique: I don't know of any other firm that has an onsite expert (who, bald and seventy-three years old, looks the part!) to walk clients through the Medicare maze. Most financial advisors and firms avoid selling Medicare supplements or providing any advice because the time and expertise don't translate into big revenue. It's a low-margin business, similar to the way some physicians don't accept Medicare because their reimbursement rates are less than private insurance.

LIFE INSURANCE

Retirees are not the target market for life insurance. You're no longer protecting an income stream or providing for dependents. You've already gone through the wealth accumulation phase, and now you just have to hold on to your nest egg. You're probably pretty close to paying off your house if you haven't already. Nevertheless, it's good to understand the basics of life insurance, which for retirees can also be useful as an estate planning tool.

A life insurance policy is a contract with an insurance company. In exchange for premium payments, the insurer is obligated to pay the coverage amount to the beneficiary upon the insured's death. This death benefit is typically received by the beneficiary income tax free.

Life insurance can do the following:

- Typically provides immediate liquidity to the beneficiary or estate

- Serves as an income replacement for the surviving spouse

- Provides for education, childcare, and other needs of children

- Allows beneficiaries to eliminate debt

- Provides coverage for business owners and key executives

- Provides for other special needs

- Potentially builds cash value

It is important to understand the types of life insurance available and how each works. Life insurance can be broken into two general classifications—*term* and *permanent*.

When comparing the costs and benefits of term insurance to permanent insurance, keep in mind that despite what it may seem from the promised payoff, neither policy is too good to be true. The costs and corresponding death benefits are actuarially determined.

> While permanent insurance is typically more expensive than term insurance in the initial years of coverage, it will likely seem more and more reasonable, even inexpensive, as you get older.

While permanent insurance is typically more expensive than term insurance in the initial years of coverage, it will likely seem more and more reasonable, even inexpensive, as you get older. With this in mind, it is crucial to understand what risks you are insuring against before you select the type of insurance to purchase.

Typically, instead of permanent insurance, I'd recommend term insurance to cover a need for protection during a specific period. For example, if you have twenty years left on your mortgage, or twenty years before retirement when you need to protect an income stream, it'd make sense to purchase a twenty-year term policy. It's usually the more prudent option than cash value or permanent insurance.

Though life insurance can be a valuable component of an overall financial plan, I have my gripes with the industry as a whole. One of my biggest complaints is its aggressive sales culture and the fact that you're invariably buying a policy from a middleman who is impossible to bypass. There's always a salesperson (or three) interposed between the customer and the service, and naturally this extra cost is passed on to you.

Even I, a Chartered Life Underwriter (the highest standard; kind of the insurance equivalent of a CFP), can't go directly to Prudential and get a better rate by circumventing the middleman looking for his cut; it doesn't work like that. In the insurance industry, even if you go straight to the source (the provider), you're not going to save anything.

And some companies are simply too aggressive in their sales tactics. They often try to sell life insurance as an investment vehicle or as a wealth accumulation vehicle, but I've never seen that work well.

For example, a guy might pitch a million-dollar life insurance policy to Mr. and Mrs. Smith, age fifty. Instead of investing money in their IRAs or 401(k)s, they'll end up putting $15,000 to $20,000 per year into premiums for the policy. "It's going to build up all this cash value," Mr. Salesman breathlessly explains, for the thousandth time. "Then, you can borrow against this cash value to help pay for your children's college costs and also supplement your retirement. And guess what? When you get all this money out, because it's an insurance vehicle, it's going to be all tax free."

It sounds nice, right? Well, that's how sales pitches are supposed to sound. But phrases like "tax free," "protect your loved ones," "wealth accumulation," and "no stock market risk" (if it's not a variable policy) are just bait to lure in unsuspecting fish. What they don't tell you is that the cash value historically has accumulated at rates much lower than market returns—usually 3 to 5 percent, instead of 7 to 10 percent in the market. In addition, when you begin withdrawals of the cash value from the policy, the insurance company typically considers it a loan against the policy, and the rates they charge for these loans can be as high as 8 percent. So you're earning 4 percent on the cash value while borrowing at 8 percent, plus you have the cost of the insurance itself. And I would never suggest using it to pay for college or some other type of expense during your working years.

These policies can end up being upside down in a hurry, kind of like someone who buys a car and makes payments over eight years. By year five they want to trade in their vehicle and realize they have to pay a lot of money just to walk away from it!

Buy insurance for protection but not as an investment.

For retirees, life insurance does have some advantages for estate planning. It can be subject to estate taxes (if not held in an irrevocable life insurance trust), but it is received income tax free. That's another perk if you're looking to bequeath its value. However, since Congress has hiked the estate tax threshold so high, there's less pressure to use life insurance as an estate planning tool. At TFA, it's a very small part of our business.

LONG-TERM CARE INSURANCE

While life insurance is designed to protect against a catastrophic event that renders you unable to care for your family or pay the mortgage, in retirement, the catastrophic event everyone fears is becoming unable to care for yourself. When you're sixty-five and healthy, it's still hard to really believe it'll happen to you, but almost 70 percent of retirees will need long-term care at some point. And twenty percent will need it for five years or more.[16]

With long-term care insurance, you're buying it for yourself, but you're also buying it for those around you, because it provides them peace of mind that no matter what, you're going to get good, pro-

---

16   "How Much Care Will You Need?" LongTermCare.gov, 2017, https://long-termcare.acl.gov/the-basics/how-much-care-will-you-need.html https://longtermcare.acl.gov/the-basics/how-much-care-will-you-need.html.

fessional care. Often, the greatest gift you can give your children is letting them rest easy in the knowledge that they won't have to take care of aging parents. And it's hopefully going to protect a legacy for your heirs, since out-of-pocket nursing home costs can decimate one's savings.

When purchasing a plan, make sure you understand these key terms:

- *Daily Benefit*: Policies are limited to a specified amount per day (example: $150/day). All other factors being equal, the higher the daily coverage, the more expensive the policy will be.

- *Elimination Period*: Policies contain an elimination period (example: 30–180 days) before the insurance coverage begins payment of benefits. The shorter the elimination period, the more expensive the policy will be.

- *Duration*: Policies will specify how long the benefits will be paid by the insurance company. The duration can typically range from two years up to the insured's lifetime. The longer the duration of benefits payable, the more expensive the policy will be.

- *COLA*: A policy that provides a cost of living adjustment (COLA) allows your benefit amount to increase over time with inflation. Adding a COLA to your policy will increase the cost, as it increases the level of protection.

- *Riders*: A policy may offer additional coverage for additional cost.

- *Tax Qualified*: Certain policies may receive favorable tax benefits provided premiums exceed 7.5 percent of the insured's AGI when combined with other unreimbursed medical expenses. The amount of the 2020 premium deduction is subject to IRS limits by age.

I don't recommend long-term care insurance for everyone. If you're sufficiently wealthy (say, $2 million in liquid net worth), you can self-insure by paying for those expenses out of pocket. It's the people who are in the $500,000 to $2 million range who really need it, since paying for long-term care out of their own funds will put a huge dent in (if not drain!) their portfolios. You didn't save your whole life just to spend your twilight years lining the pockets of a nursing home CEO.

Then again, by the same logic, if you're affluent, you can probably afford the premiums anyway.

Generally, for a sixty-year-old couple, any kind of decent coverage will cost $5,000 to $7,000 a year that they will be paying for the rest of their lives for insurance that they may not need. And that cost is likely to go up over time. That might be 10 percent of their retirement budget, maybe more. And some people say, "Would I rather take a nice vacation each year or pay this long-term care insurance premium? I'd rather take the vacations, then in the last six months of my life move to Oregon, where assisted suicide is legal."

> Long-term care is such a staggering cost that for some, death starts to look like the better option!

I'm not joking—I've been hearing clients say that more and more over the last few years. Long-term care is such a staggering cost that for some, death starts to look like the better option!

For most of our clients, a two- to four-year stay in a nursing home without insurance usually won't break the bank, especially if it happens when they're in their eighties or nineties and near the end of their lives. It becomes a problem when somebody needs care much earlier and for an extended period of time—for example, someone who develops early onset dementia at sixty-seven and lives for another ten years with constant care. At $8,000 a month or so, that's going to run them a million bucks.

Even if you do have insurance, a protracted stay is problematic because insurance policies typically cover only three to five years. When insurance runs out, you're basically on your own, left to spend down your assets. When you have almost nothing left, you'll qualify for Medicaid—but only if you're destitute, with around $2,000 in assets (not counting the value of your house).

When you look at these grim prospects, whether insured or not, and whether you end up using the policy or not, it seems like a lose-lose.

At TFA, client interest in long-term care insurance has declined over the last half decade. Part of it is because of premium increases. Another reason is that the underwriting has become much more stringent, and the insurance companies keep finding ways to preclude people because of things like diabetes. The strength of the stock market has also probably been a factor—people have been getting such blockbuster growth in their portfolios that they're more confident in their ability to pay for care with their own assets.

This trend reflects a general contraction in the long-term care insurance market. When I got into the business in the late '90s, there were a hundred different insurance carriers offering it. Now, it's down to around ten. It's just not as profitable as it once was. The industry has mispriced premiums dramatically, and people are living longer and needing long-term care insurance more often. And with interest rates so low, the insurance companies haven't been able to earn the money on the premiums that they had projected.

There is another option that more of our clients have chosen over the last decade: a hybrid policy that contains both long-term care insurance and life insurance. They can pay a lump sum premium and purchase a bucket of long-term care coverage for a specific period of time. If they never need to use the long-term care insurance, an insurance death benefit is paid income tax free to their beneficiary that's approximately equivalent to the lump sum they paid to purchase the policy in the first place.

In effect, they are buying some peace of mind. They hope they never *need* long-term care, but they have it just in case. If they are fortunate to never need it, their beneficiary gets the money back in the form of a death benefit.

WHAT MATTERS IN LIFE

I'm wrestling with a lot of these questions myself as my siblings and I try to figure out how to care for my aging parents. Now that their health isn't as good as it used to be, they need some help at home a few times a week. I think they acknowledge this need, but they're still fighting me on it. Mom and Dad are proud people, and it's hard for anybody to go from being self-reliant their whole lives to having a stranger come into their home and assist them with daily tasks. I keep having to remind them that they shouldn't feel like they have to entertain the person; her job is to help them get their day started, make sure they're eating right and taking their medications, make sure they don't fall, and so on. Or just make sure they don't lie on the couch all day and eat a dozen Snickers bars.

My family has certainly been through our share of medical travails. If not for insurance, as well as Medicaid, we'd probably be bankrupt. When my daughter was born fourteen weeks premature, it kicked off a battery of intensive round-the-clock care in the NICU, replete with blood tests, ultrasounds, intravenous fluids, and a whole bevy of monitors and machines. Of course, when it's all happening, costs are the last thing on your mind, but after four months in the NICU, my daughter was a million-dollar baby.

We were eminently grateful that Medicaid paid for it all. That's because if your child is born weighing under 1,200 grams—about two and a half pounds—Medicaid covers everything through the Low Birth Weight Program. I remember seeing the bills coming in and then seeing "balance due: zero" and thinking, "Holy cow. How would somebody handle this without Medicaid?" And I also felt a little guilty thinking about how much it would cost the system. But programs like Medicaid and Medicare are there to provide much-needed help for Americans—both the very old and the very young.

Of course, what really counts are the big, emotional questions under the surface of the financial calculations. Not just "How does this affect our net worth" but "How does this affect *us*?"

My client Mark is one of the brightest guys you'll ever meet. Tall and scholarly, he is a former university president, and he looks the part. He has an authoritative bearing, but he's low key and sociable. He's been a client of ours for six years, having chosen TFA after interviewing with eight different financial advisors.

Mark is enjoying retirement with Vanessa, his wife of fifty years, despite the daily challenges that come with Parkinson's disease, which Mark was diagnosed with a few years ago. It's tough to see. Parkinson's is progressive, meaning it gets worse over time. And it's taken an immense toll on both his and his wife's well-being. It's agonizing for her to see a spouse struggle like that. The truth is that being a caregiver of a sick person exacts a great mental and physical toll.

Nevertheless, both Mark and Vanessa are strong, stoic, and realistic about the whole situation. He accepts his mortality and just wants to make sure everything is taken care of. When the diagnosis came, it radically altered his financial plan. We went from scrutinizing rates of return and portfolio allocation to just making sure he would have the care and insurance he needed while providing a financial cushion for his wife and being able to leave something behind for his kids.

A lot of the conversations I have with retirees revolve around "How much can I do now while I'm still able, as opposed to later?" It's better to give with warm hands than cold hands. Mark and Vanessa, for example, have decided to give the maximum annual gifts to their four children ($15,000 per spouse) for the next five years. They are incredibly happy to do this while they are both living and at a time when their kids need and greatly appreciate the gift.

No one likes to think about death, much less their own, but it's a reality that we all have to face. Later in life, that reality becomes more immediate, if not imminent. But maintaining control of your finances in the face of serious and expensive life-changing illness can be life affirming. Spending your hard-earned money on things that bring you joy—whether it's an unforgettable vacation or helping your adult children get a foothold in the world—beats back death and reminds you that you're still the master of your fate, that your life is your own until the very end. It's a way of affirming, "I might be old, I might be ailing—but

> No one likes to think about death, much less their own, but it's a reality that we all have to face. Later in life, that reality becomes more immediate, if not imminent.

I'm still here, and I won't let anything stop me from doing the things I always imagined I would."

TAKEAWAYS:

1. If you are considering life insurance, choose term life insurance that is good for a specific period of time when you really need to protect your earning potential.

2. Retiring early? Then formulate a plan for your healthcare needs ahead of time. Before Medicare kicks in at sixty-five, you'll need coverage; without it, you're walking a tightrope. A major medical emergency or long-term illness can devastate your finances.

3. Most elderly Americans will need long-term care insurance at some point. Even so, you should account for the possibility of very long-term care (more than five years). If the insurance benefits run out, do you have enough to pay your expenses? If not, what will you do? Wait until your assets are spent and then use Medicaid? Rely on family members? Be aware of the risks and plan accordingly.

CHAPTER EIGHT

CHARITABLE GIVING IN RETIREMENT

A nyone who has been through the ordeal of their child being born premature can tell you about the whirlwind of emotions they endure. Long sleepless nights in the NICU will rattle your psyche and leave you feeling helpless, and such helplessness is especially difficult because your parental instinct ignites a powerful will to fix things: you'd move mountains for your little baby, but there's not much you can actually do except try to keep your spirits up and trust the doctors and nurses will help your newborn pull through.

Christina and I remain eternally grateful to our friends, family, and colleagues, whose support helped alleviate that feeling of helplessness. Families who find themselves in a similar situation can also take solace in the fact that there are whole organizations that advocate tirelessly for moms and babies. The March of Dimes is one group that for more than eighty years has dedicated itself to, among other things, helping women achieve safe pregnancies and providing access to neonatal care. In the last few years, my family and I have become proud active supporters of the March of Dimes.

Volunteerism was something I came to later in life. For most of my adult life, I'd wanted to get involved in a cause, but I could never quite find my niche. I think a lot of people feel that way too—they want to give back somehow, but they haven't yet discovered how and where to direct their energy and talents to make an impact. For me, the March of Dimes proved to be the initiative I had always been looking for.

We have partnered with the March of Dimes to cohost its two primary local events that are held annually here in Greensboro: the March for Babies and the Signature Chefs Auction. My firm is underwriting the cost of both of these events for the next three years so that 100 percent of every dollar raised at them will go directly toward fighting prematurity and helping mothers.

The March for Babies is a walkathon that raises money for research into infant mortality, premature births, and birth defects. Havana; our twin boys, Walker and Quincy; Christina; and I all take part. It's not just the Rush clan: our fundraising cadre also includes Havana's friends from school, our neighbors, my employees, and other friends and associates in Greensboro. It's touching to see how many people show up and support us and thrilling to raise so much money for such an important cause. For years, our team has been the top fundraiser for the local March of Babies walk.

The Signature Chefs event is a black-tie shindig during which local chefs and restaurants auction off dining experiences and home visits where they prepare a meal in your own kitchen. One year the local TV news affiliate sent out a reporter, and Christina, Havana, and I got to share our story about Havana's dramatic birth and how it inspired us to get involved in the organization.

I've served as chairman for the event, and TFA is one of the major sponsors of the Signature Chefs gala, as March of Dimes has asked me a number of times to deliver the opening remarks. Public speaking is something I enjoy, but it was a little difficult at first to talk candidly about something so personal as Havana's birth, about the tumultuous days in the NICU while our daughter was fighting for her life.

I realized when I sat down to compose my speech that there were still a lot of emotions that I hadn't fully processed. When you're going through something like that, you don't even really have time to dwell on what's happening; you just put the blinders on and press forward, day by day, hour by hour, second by second.

So as my pen tangoed across the notepad, the real, raw emotions came to the surface again. It was therapeutic to sift through those feelings and put them into words. And there's no audience more receptive or empathetic than the March of Dimes crowd.

In addition, we recently completed a new initiative with the March of Dimes called "Points for Preemies." Since my kids and I thoroughly enjoy University of North Carolina Greensboro basketball and attend every home game, we decided to donate $1 to the March of Dimes for every point the UNCG basketball team scored.

This chapter isn't just to plug the March of Dimes. I'm going to tell you how you can combine your passion for a cause with smart tax and investment advice that will save you money and benefit the charities of your choice. Charitable giving is important at any stage of life, and just because you're retired doesn't mean you have to cut back.

> Charitable giving is important at any stage of life, and just because you're retired doesn't mean you have to cut back.

DONOR-ADVISED FUNDS

As an advisor, few things give me a greater sense of professional satisfaction than doing well by my clients by helping them grow their wealth and live their dreams. But I also strongly believe that there is a social responsibility that comes with a high level of financial success: gain big and give back. There are ways of fulfilling that responsibility that are fiscally prudent.

Donor-advised funds (DAFs) are a tax-efficient way of giving to charity. A DAF is a personal charitable account opened in the name of one or more individual donors and held in custody by a nonprofit organization. This nonprofit could be a community foundation, university, or charitable organization founded by a financial services company—basically any IRS-qualified public charity. The account is managed by nonprofit "sponsoring organizations" (like a Community Foundation or Schwab Charitable), but the donor (i.e., you) has say over when and how much to contribute.

Some high-net-worth individuals consider starting a family foundation or charitable trust to pursue their philanthropic goals, but that involves a lot of administrative costs, mandatory reporting procedures, and other red tape. The comparative simplicity of the DAF is one of its benefits.

Using DAFs for charitable giving has been tremendously popular with our clients, who naturally also appreciate the significant tax deductions a DAF furnishes. Save money *and* benefit a worthy cause—that's a win-win for all parties.

Here's how it works: let's say there's a donor who writes a $10,000 check to their church each year. They're paying for that with after-tax money, and that $10,000 might not even be deductible because the standard deduction is now much higher than it used to be thanks to tax code changes.

But this donor also has $50,000 in Apple stock they've been holding on to for a long time. If they sell it, it's going to trigger a hefty capital gains tax. Instead, they can donate the stock to a donor-advised fund as an irrevocable gift (meaning it can't be taken back). They get a $50,000 tax deduction right away, but they don't have to actually give the whole $50,000 right away—just park it in the fund.

Then, they can make periodic donations each year (as much or as little as they want)[17] according to their desired timeline.

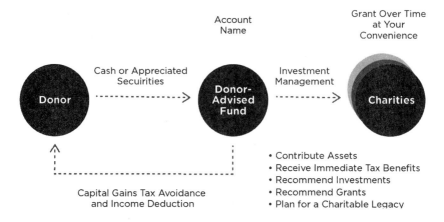

It's an excellent way to reduce your taxable income while maintaining control of your charitable giving.

Importantly, the capital in the DAF can be invested by the sponsoring organization and continue to grow. Because of the strength of the market, some of our clients have seen their funds grow in value even as they're making distributions each year to charity. That's been the case with Dan and Patricia, two of our clients who have built up an impressive fund. Some years ago, they vowed to save a million dollars in their DAF by the time they retired so that they could continue to give generously in their later years. Thus far, the $725,000 they've invested in the DAF has ballooned to $1.15 million. Thanks to strong market performance, they're donating $50,000 a year, and they haven't even reached retirement yet.

At TFA, we're such proponents of donor-advised funds that we don't charge management fees to set them up and oversee them. We feel the societal benefit makes it worth our time. As an advisor, it's

---

17 Technically, there are minimums, but they're negligible. For a $50,000 account, it would be something like $50 a year the donor has to give away.

rewarding when you can present a solution that is both community minded and financially savvy. It also encourages people who might ordinarily not be so charitable to participate. A DAF lets you continue to support valuable causes without tapping into your 401(k), IRA, brokerage account, or portfolio paycheck income.

QUALIFIED CHARITABLE DISTRIBUTIONS

I'm always pleased to meet with Mary, one of our most generous clients. Mary is a well-dressed, diminutive woman with a warm smile and a penchant for organization. You can tell she was an executive assistant before retiring because she always asks for a copy of our notetaker's notes after every meeting!

After diligently saving over the years, Mary and her late husband had accumulated over $1 million in both an individual account and a retirement account. Once Mary retired, she wanted to make sure that she was as income tax efficient in retirement as she had been during her working years.

When Mary reached age 70½, we began taking distributions from her IRA as required by the IRS (the age has since been changed to 72). Since the RMDs were a new source of taxable income, we decided to use qualified charitable distributions (QCD) to decrease her taxable income *and* maintain her longstanding philanthropic habits while still satisfying the RMD requirement.

QCD is a charitable giving tax strategy available to investors over the age of 70½ and is especially attractive to individuals who have reached the RMD age of 72. If you've accumulated a lot of money in these accounts, this often means you're forced to withdraw way more than you actually need.

This tax stratagem is a win-win-win option for those who are celebrating seventy-two trips around the sun. When Mary reached the RMD age, she did not change her charitable giving habits, only the way in which she gifted. Mary and I arranged for a check to be written to the charity of her choice from her IRA. Since the check was made payable to the charity itself, the distribution was not taxed. It still qualified as part of Mary's RMD, yet the amount donated to charity is not taxable income. Hence, Mary was able to satisfy part of her RMD (win number one) without having to pay taxes on the distribution (win number two). And charities that are in good standing as a 501(c)(3) do not pay taxes on donations they receive (win number three).

Another advantage (win number four) of this method is that by reducing your taxable income, you might avoid paying the higher Medicare surcharge if you're in an upper-income bracket. QCDs are an "above the line" deduction, *not* an itemized deduction. Therefore, these donations reduce your adjusted gross income. They are capped at $100,000 per year, but that's a lot of money that could have a big effect on a nonprofit.

> At TFA, we're big on donor-advised funds and qualified charitable distributions because our community spirit is an essential part of who we are as a firm.

IT'S NOT JUST ABOUT THE MONEY

At TFA, we're big on donor-advised funds and qualified charitable distributions because our community spirit is an essential part of who we are as a firm.

We recently were part of an inaugural award given by the Invest in Others Charitable Foundation, which recognized twenty advisory firms across the country for their philanthropic work and for creating a culture of philanthropy within their companies, and it designated us an "Invest in Others Champion." In many ways, this was more special to me than being recognized as a top advisor by *Barron's*, *Forbes*, or the *Financial Times*. And in 2020, I'm currently in the process of working toward a new designation called the Chartered Advisor in Philanthropy. I believe this will be helpful personally and professionally.

The March of Dimes is TFA's flagship initiative, but we're involved in other programs too. My predecessor at TFA was one of the founding members of a group called Women to Women, which is an all-female grant-making endowment that supports various women-focused causes, from support for victims of domestic violence to promoting economic security for mothers. TFA remains a major sponsor of the group, and our company has enthusiastically covered the $2,500 donation fee required for lifetime membership for eight of our female employees so that they can contribute to this excellent group. We are also the Presenting Sponsor for the group's annual luncheon, which over a thousand people attend to show their support for the local community.

We're also proud supporters of the United Way of Greensboro, whose Family Success Center helps down-on-their-luck individuals and families. One of the barriers to low-income people getting back on their feet is mobility: if you don't have a car or if public transportation is spotty, it's difficult to travel from place to place to access services you need, attend job interviews, and so on. TFA supports the Family Success Center's clients by sponsoring gas cards and bus cards to alleviate this burden.

Each December, you can also find our employees ringing bells for the Salvation Army Christmas fundraiser. Some of our clients get involved too, which is awesome, and my family turns out as well. Havana, Quincy, and Walker have been eager participants since they were three years old. It's important to me to inculcate these values in my children. It's never too early to learn to be grateful for what you have and to express that gratitude by giving something back.

That's also why I'm so enthusiastic about getting clients to combine their altruistic side with their financial savvy via donor-advised funds and QCD. In truth, for a lot of advisors, setting up a donor-advised fund is too much headache for too little money, so they just don't do it. But we think it's the right thing to do, for both the community's sake and for that of the client.

TAKEAWAYS:

1. Donor-advised funds give you a tax write-off and let you maintain a measure of control over the disbursement of funds, even as the charitable organization administers the account and determines how it's invested. (On this latter point, there are exceptions. For a DAF held by a financial services company like Charles Schwab, you keep control of how it's invested.)

2. If you are taking sizable required minimum withdrawals and have an interest in contributing more to charity, qualified charitable distributions can kill two birds with one stone.

CHAPTER NINE

TALKING WITH YOUR FAMILY ABOUT MONEY

I don't actually ever remember having a conversation about money with my parents as a kid, beyond asking them for lunch money for the week. Heck, it probably wasn't until I was in college that we really discussed the subject. I know our family was hardly alone in this—many families shy away from the topic, to their own detriment.

For anyone, and for retirees in particular, open and honest discussions with children, parents, and spouses is an important part of financial planning.

TALKING WITH YOUR KIDS

Some families are good at going over money matters. For others, it's a taboo topic.

Maybe you're fretting that discussing finances will be the most uncomfortable conversation you've had with your kids since the dreaded facts of life talk when they were younger. However, it doesn't have to be unpleasant. In fact, dialoguing about serious financial issues that are essential to your family's well-being can bring a welcome feeling of levity.

> Dialoguing about serious financial issues that are essential to your family's well-being can bring a welcome feeling of levity.

If you're a retiree, the discussion with your adult kids typically revolves around two main considerations: (1) will you have enough to live comfortably and be taken care of, even if your health fails, and (2) whether, how, and how much of your wealth do you intend to share, either in life in the form of a gift or as an inheritance?

The greatest blessing an aging parent can give their kids is the assurance that they won't be a burden. Needless to say, out-of-pocket healthcare costs (especially long-term care for the infirm) can be astronomical. Some people assume their folks will be taken care of by Medicaid, but you won't be eligible until you're basically destitute. Families who opt to care for their elderly parents at home can save money, but there is a tremendous emotional cost to being a caregiver.

Apart from healthcare expenses, children want to know that their retired parents' month-to-month spending won't outstrip their budget. They see Mom and Dad are living it up, perhaps for the first time in their adult lives, and worry their spending is profligate.

If you're in good financial shape, reassure your kids that you have plenty to keep wining and dining and golfing and globe-trotting without having to fret about running out of funds by the time you reach your golden years.

The opposite question of "Will my parents have enough?" is "If they have so much, can they siphon some off to me?" Adult children who realize that their parents are sitting on a fortune can get a little covetous. Obviously, how much (or little) a parent wants to give to their children is entirely up to them, and each family deals with this in their own way. For married couples, IRS rules allow for each spouse to gift as much as $15,000 each year to as many individuals as they like, so technically, a husband and wife could together give $30,000 each year to each of their children (or friends, nieces, nephews, etc.) without having to file a gift tax return.

It's not uncommon for children to start asking for more than their parents feel comfortable giving, and that puts the parents in an awkward spot, since of course every mother and father's first instinct is to provide the best possible life for their offspring. In my experience, the kids' requests vary from essential to self-indulgent. Maybe it's help with paying off major credit card debt. Maybe it's something more luxurious (some might say frivolous), like joining a country club. I myself could never imagine asking my parents to finance a country club membership, but I've seen it happen.

Some parents struggle with telling their children no—the protective instinct kicking in. In that case, they might turn to us to play bad cop to their good cop and gently but firmly remind their children that it's Mom and Dad's money, and they're entitled to do what they want with it, even if that means enjoying a lavish and indulgent retirement. After all, they've earned it.

The best way to assuage your children's concern, whether it's their worry that you'll go bankrupt or their frustration that they're not getting as big a slice of pie as they feel entitled to, is to have frank conversations about the subject. Manage expectations and set boundaries.

Most parents want their progeny to learn to stand on their own two feet. Affluent retirees, particularly those who are self-made, got that way through a strong work ethic, and they understand that merely giving your child of any age what they want is counterproductive in the long run.

A couple of my favorite clients, Andrew and Ariana, really put this principle into practice. They're the quintessential immigrants-making-it-in-America success story: he moved from Jamaica with his family at an early age, and she hails from the Philippines. Andrew graduated from Columbia and went on to become a physician, which is how he met Ariana, who's a nurse.

The combined income of two hardworking medical professionals have allowed them to build a sizable nest egg, but despite their affluence, they live extremely frugally. I've met many doctors whose splashy lifestyles and expensive tastes inhibit their financial planning. But Andrew and Ariana aren't like that at all. They're also heavily involved in several community initiatives, which is another testament to their good character.

Unsurprisingly, they're intent on instilling their children with the same spirit of self-reliance that made them successful. So their estate documents explicitly dictate that their children will not inherit their assets until the kids are sixty years old—even if one or both of the parents dies long before that. That's how much they're opposed to financing their children's lifestyles or gifting them an early retirement.

It's not miserliness—it's a good-faith desire to pass on the right values. After all, an inheritance can be spent down quickly, but a strong work ethic will stay with you for life. That kind of blue-collar ethos resonates with me, and I think Andrew and Ariana's children will be grateful for their parents' foresight.

On the flip side, some parents may have a goal to allow their children the ability to follow their passions in life without being burdened by money. Perhaps the child wants to be an artist or pursue their entrepreneurial spirit in a business idea. The parents want to support this and don't want to wait until after they die to see their children realize their goals and dreams. Again, this is where a good financial advisor needs to listen to their clients and identify their goals and intentions. We may not agree personally or professionally with providing the proverbial silver spoon to children, but our job is to show our clients how to turn dreams into realities by pulling the right levers with a disciplined financial plan and investing strategy.

TALKING WITH YOUR SPOUSE/PARTNER

Just as it's important for children and parents to have a dialogue about finances, spouses must also be on the same page. This seems obvious, but many couples fall short at financial communication, which is especially risky as they age into retirement.

This is particularly the case for couples for whom finances are the exclusive domain of one spouse, while the other remains in the dark. We generally discourage that kind of arrangement; both parties must be informed, which is why when we schedule meetings at the office, we urge both spouses to attend. We also strive to make sure married women feel listened to and treated as equals since traditionally, wives have been marginalized in financial planning.

Successful marriages tend to involve an efficient division of labor, where one spouse handles *X* and the other deals with *Y*, so it's okay if one person takes the lead in financial planning, as long as the other still knows what's going. In my own household, Christina has ceded this responsibility to me (rumor has it that I know a thing or two about the subject), but I'm diligent about keeping her abreast of financial concerns, especially with regard to essential documents, where our accounts are kept, whom to contact in the event of an emergency, and so on.

> **Even if someone is not fully engaged in the day-to-day, down-and-dirty details of financial planning, they must have a basic level of financial literacy and must be prepared if tragedy strikes and their spouse is incapacitated or dies.**

Even if someone is not fully engaged in the day-to-day, down-and-dirty details of financial planning, they must have a basic level of financial literacy and must be prepared if tragedy strikes and their spouse is incapacitated or dies.

I'm dealing with this scenario right now with a pair of clients. Fred and Maggie are both in their midseventies. Last week Maggie called me and uttered the words everyone dreads having to say: "My husband is in the ER now. He has a brain aneurysm, and in a few hours he's going into surgery. What do I do?"

On top of fretting about her husband's health, she was scared out of her mind about having to suddenly deal with various financial concerns that he's handled during fifty-plus years of marriage. Not just the major stuff, like wills and retirement accounts, but the mundane stuff, like paying bills on time.

It's terrible to have this responsibility abruptly forced upon you at the moment when you're least prepared emotionally to deal with it.

But I told Maggie that she had nothing to worry about, since we had it covered. We had all the insurance, advance medical directives, direct deposits, and everything else already taken care of and all the essential documents at our fingertips.

We've since had several meetings with Fred and Maggie's children, one of whom has power of attorney for her father. We brought them into the conversations because they needed to understand the financial plan and reassure their mother. They have transitioned their father into nursing care, while their mother is moving into an adjacent independent living home at the continuing care retirement community.

For an advisor, it's nice to be able to reassure a distraught client (and her children) that she can focus her attention on her husband's recovery. Nevertheless, the more self-reliant you can be, the better.

Another situation where there might be a spousal communication disconnect is between couples who are in their second or third marriages and who have chosen to keep their finances separate. In such cases, we might be working with only one spouse or working with both but maintaining the financial separation.

Obviously, running two separate financial plans presents more challenges than maintaining just one, though in my experience, remarried couples who have chosen not to combine their financial lives are happy with the decision.

The key caveat is that even if their financial plans and accounts remain separate, *they must be on the same page about their intentions.* And that, again, is just a matter of candid communication. For example, if you're both in your second marriage but you each have children from a first marriage, how will you handle your estate(s)? Who are the chosen beneficiaries? Things like that can get very tricky.

Rachel and Sal are an interesting case. She is seventy-nine, and he's a few years younger. They have a combined net worth of a couple million dollars, but Sal actually has very little himself; almost all the assets are in Rachel's name. A big chunk of that comes from a generous inheritance she's barely touched since receiving it years ago.

But lately, Sal has taken a sudden and rather suspicious interest in getting access to her funds. Since they're in her name, we can't dole out a penny without her permission. And I know from conversations with her that she's not comfortable with her husband having unfettered access to her accounts. The fact that she's also showing signs of dementia makes the situation more worrisome because it puts her in a vulnerable state.

Not long ago, Sal showed up and demanded we give him $30,000 from her account so he could "pay his friend's attorney fees" (which in itself seems odd). It got weirder though. A couple of weeks after this unannounced visit, Sal and Rachel returned with a handful of dubious legal documents—basically, templates he downloaded from the internet—including a power of attorney. I could see they weren't valid, but it was still disconcerting.

Being a financial advisor means you're a lot more than just a spreadsheet-obsessed "numbers guy"; you develop an acute intuition for human behavior. Something about Sal and Rachel's interaction seemed off. It seemed she was being pressured into being there. The way he spoke a little too forcefully and touched her a little too aggressively set off alarm bells in my head. Even though he had brought a stack of (questionable) legal documents into my office, she seemed reluctant to give him sweeping oversight of her finances.

We don't meddle in private affairs, but as a fiduciary, we have to be attuned to situations that seem untoward. And we can't just sit there and let this husband withdraw whatever he wants whenever he wants, change the beneficiaries on the account, and so forth. He seemed to be taking advantage of his wife's fragile mental state.

This situation is still evolving, but now an attorney is involved, and a guardianship hearing for Rachel has been scheduled. Sal continues to try to take large sums of money from her accounts because he wants to travel to Europe (without his wife). The attorney is asking for one of my advisors to testify at the guardianship hearing because the advisor has intimate knowledge of Rachel's wishes regarding her assets before incapacitation.

Regardless of how it eventually concludes, this is an important cautionary tale for anyone: if you, your spouse, or your parent is showing signs of cognitive decline, you need to have a candid talk about it, particularly about the potential effect on finances. Unfortunately, we see this a lot in our business, especially as our clientele is aging into their seventies, eighties, and beyond. There's really only so much an advisor can legally and practically do to intervene in such situations; you must advocate for yourself or your loved ones.

My friend Peter, for example, started noticing something wasn't quite right with his elderly mother. It wasn't just routine absent-mindedness—she seemed to be having trouble remembering basic things, her sharp verbal acuity had dulled, and clutter had invaded her normally tidy abode.

Peter drops by her place several times a week, and during one visit, he noticed a growing sprawl of unopened mail slowly taking over the kitchen table.

"What's all this, Ma?" he asked.

"I don't know," she said. "Just junk, I guess." But in that pile Peter found uncashed checks, unpaid bills, and, most concerning of all, past-due letters from his mother's long-term care insurance company.

Imagine paying premiums for ten or twenty years in preparation for the day when you might need long-term care, only to find that the company has dropped you because you missed a few billing cycles. A lapsed policy is usually worthless; in many cases, the insurance company has no obligation to provide care. Some policies do come with an "unintended lapse provision" that provides some protection against this scenario, but otherwise, it's a nightmare scenario that, for those with age-induced cognitive decline, tends to emerge at the exact moment when they might soon be needing long-term care.

Peter realized that he had to get more involved in his mother's financial life, so he brought her to us, and we helped straighten out the tangled mess of multiple accounts, dividends, and bills—and we made sure the right insurance was still in place. It was tough for Peter (as it would be for any of us) to confront his mother about this situation and acknowledge the harsh truth about her declining mental state, but doing so probably saved her from financial ruin, quite literally.

At TFA, we also ask clients if there is a third party (usually a son or daughter) whom we can contact if we're ever concerned the client is somehow under undue pressure (like Rachel), is being scammed, or is showing signs of cognitive impairment that would jeopardize their ability to manage their finances.

It doesn't mean we divulge specifics about their private financial data, but it allows us to fulfill our fiduciary duty by contacting a trusted individual to ask, "Hey, is everything okay with your dad? He's been acting a little out of sorts lately."

You must be vigilant—and that means being vigilant about your advisor too. Not all advisors are on the up-and-up. In our office, children of elderly clients sometimes join in on meetings, just to keep an eye on things. I appreciate this, since I understand the risks involved and how much is at stake. And I know that while they may be few in number, there are indeed unscrupulous advisors who would take advantage of their elderly clients' mental fragility. It's an unfortunate reality. Just protect yourself. Communicating with family is the best defense.

CHECKLISTS:

Here are some questions to ask your parents:

- *When do you plan to retire?*
- *How will you spend your time in retirement?*
- *Do you plan to stay in the same house, or will you move? This broaches the important question of where the parent intends to live: independently, with their children, in a continuing care retirement community, and so on.*
- *Do you feel financially secure? Are you working with a financial advisor?*
- *Do you have life insurance and long-term care insurance?*
- *Do you have your legal documents in order—power of attorney (financial and medical), will or trust, advance healthcare directive (living will), and so on? Do you have beneficiaries listed on your 401(k) s, IRAs, life insurance, and so on?*
- *On that note, is there anything in your estate plan that you think may cause friction among beneficiaries, such as siblings?*
- *If you eventually need long-term care assistance,*

how will you handle it?

- *If something were to happen to you, do you have a place where we could easily locate all your important documents and the necessary people to contact?*

Here are some questions to ask if you're expecting to receive an inheritance from your folks:

- *What does this money mean to you, and how can I be a good steward of this money?*
- *How do you envision this inheritance benefiting me and potentially future generations?*
- *Is there anything this money should not be used for?*
- *Is there a particular person or firm you trust and recommend I work with to help me manage these dollars?*

VALUES, NOT NUMBERS

Ultimately, talking about finances is not a matter of discussing how much you have or don't have but about analyzing how money intersects with your goals and values. Money is a means, not the end itself. As you speak with your family, orient the discussion around what money means to you and how it allows you to be more intentionally focused on the things that can fulfill you and make your life more satisfying. Your children and/or spouse will be thankful for having the conversation. And I'm confident you'll thank yourself too.

TAKEAWAYS:

1. You don't have to divulge specific figures about your wealth, but do reassure your children that you have enough to live happily during retirement. Your advisor can, at your behest, also be involved in this family conversation, if it makes things easier.

2. Be prepared to fend off requests for money from your adult children, especially if you have a high net worth. Not everyone's kids ask for gifts, but I've seen it happen a lot. Be willing to say no if the requests are excessive or frivolous. It's your money; you get to spend it as you wish.

CHAPTER TEN

PICKING THE RIGHT ADVISOR

A dvisors are more than just retirement and investment consultants; they're lifelong advocates. A good one will stick by you for decades to help you grow your money, achieve your dreams, and live life with intention. A bad one imperils your and your family's livelihood and jeopardizes your future plans.

Unfortunately, between the sheer number of advisors and the abundance of alphabet-soup acronyms (CFA, ChFC, CIMA, FRM) bedecking their business cards, it's challenging to pick the right one for you. And many are actually better salespeople than they are advisors, which is tricky because it means they're probably also skilled at making themselves out to be more qualified than they actually are.

Who can you trust, and how do you know you're getting the service you deserve?

WORK ONLY WITH CFPS

This is one simple rule that helps you separate the wheat from the chaff: make sure your advisor is a Certified Financial Planner. It's the gold standard that differentiates qualified, credentialed professionals from self-appointed hucksters. Unlike many three- and four-letter honorifics, the CFP means something: would-be CFPs must undergo rigorous education, complete thousands of hours of on-the-job experience, pass a tough examination, and abide by a strict code of ethics. And they must renew their certification periodically, so they can't just earn the title and slack off for the next thirty years.

Surprisingly, only about a quarter of advisors, wealth managers, and planners have earned the CFP designation. You wouldn't go to a doctor if they didn't go to medical school. But for some reason, people seek financial advice from somebody who hasn't at least earned the CFP.

Some of the other common titles do carry a certain amount of prestige, but many are more marketing flash than substance. There are even firms that create their own certifications with a very low barrier to entry—like a fifty-question quiz their brokers can take on their lunch break. It's highly confusing to the regular investor out there.

Work only with CFPs, though bear in mind that being certified is only one criterion among several to assess. Just because someone is a CFP does not mean they are right for you.

In addition, the CFP should have experience working with an investor like *you*, someone who understands where you're coming from and can relate to you on a personal level. It cracks me up that our industry is dominated by men who tend to be overconfident in their ability to service the needs of widows, divorced women, and women in general.

At TFA, we take great pride in the fact that the majority of our advisors are female, and we ensure that female investors are listened to as dutifully during meetings as their male counterparts.

VETTING QUESTIONS FOR A NEW ADVISOR

1. *Does your firm participate in any revenue-sharing agreements with other investment companies?*

2. *Do you or your firm make any commission on any particular investment vehicles?*

3. *Have you or your firm ever been subject to any disciplinary action and/or fine by a regulatory agency like the SEC or FINRA?*

4. *Do you receive any additional or special compensation if a client uses your firm's banking and lending vehicles?*

5. *When did you complete your CFP, and is it in good standing with the CFP Board?*

6. *Do you invest in the same products or securities that you recommend to your clients?*

7. *Did you or your firm accept a government bailout in the form of a Paycheck Protection Program (PPP) loan in 2020?*

FIND SOMEONE YOU TRUST

Besides establishing that they're a CFP, the next most important question to ask yourself about your advisor is, "Do you trust them?" Are they a person of integrity? Will they always act in your best interest? And are they professional and proficient enough to manage your money wisely?

Some people are good at cultivating an aura of white-shoe prestige. Their impeccably clean office gleams with polished mahogany and smooth sandalwood. They dress snappily and speak with unswerving confidence. Their business cards would put Patrick Bateman to shame. But appearances can be deceiving.

Trust is to a large extent a matter of intuition, and I'd encourage people to follow their gut when evaluating prospective advisors. But you can also use more objective criteria to guide your decision. FINRA's BrokerCheck (https://brokercheck.finra.org/) and the SEC's Investment Advisor Public Disclosure database (https://www.advisorinfo.sec.gov/IAPD/default.aspx) document complaints against financial professionals. This publicly available data can be pretty revealing, so perform your due diligence.

> Advisors are required to disclose any fines, censures, or other regulatory action when meeting with a potential client the first time.

Also understand that advisors are required to disclose any fines, censures, or other regulatory action when meeting with a potential client the first time.

Last week, I came across an ad for a guy who teaches a similar course to our Retirement 101 seminar. I had never heard of him, so I looked him up on BrokerCheck. Sure enough, in the past three years alone, he has four pending litigations against him involving some potential major fines. One was for a million bucks; another was $750,000. Those are huge numbers in our business. That's not just a red flag. That's a giant blood-red banner that says *DANGER!* on it. And I found this information by searching a public database in twenty seconds.

Here's the thing: there's not a lot of oversight in our industry. So if someone *does* have complaints lodged against them, it's an indication that you should probably look elsewhere for someone to manage your money.

LOCAL VERSUS NATIONAL FIRMS

TFA is not a household name, at least not beyond the cozy confines of Greensboro, North Carolina. Big-box firms like Wells Fargo or Morgan Stanley have greater name recognition, and people gravitate toward brands they know. Names they might've seen during the halftime commercial break or on a billboard somewhere on the interstate. However, parking your money at one of these firms has drawbacks. (And I should know, since I've worked at some of them.)

I won't say that the big-box firms—the Walmarts of the financial services world—should be unequivocally avoided, but I do think there are advantages to doing business with a local, truly independent firm (I say "truly independent" because the meaning of that word, too, is sometimes muddled to hide a company's ties to larger entities).

For one, the culture of the major firms tends to prioritize salesmanship over service. Moreover, these companies operate on economies of scale; by consolidating many functions and services under one roof, they tend to cut corners with some of their client-friendly offerings. It might translate into a more efficient business model for them, but it doesn't yield strong customer service and individualized attention for the client. In my experience, the wire-house firms lack the high-touch, personalized (and personable) customer service that characterizes local firms.

It's probably cliché to talk about "feeling like a number rather than a person," but having your money managed by one of the major players often does relegate you to one entry in a vast, sprawling client list, rather than a human being with unique needs, fears, and dreams.

At TFA, we pride ourselves on a client-friendly, face-to-face approach that is congruent with our community-oriented nature. Our clients can walk right in to our office and have a conversation with multiple advisors. If they want to call us, they don't have to navigate a touch-tone maze of buttons to get an answer.

A perfect example of what I'm talking about happened last week, when I was conferring with a long-term client. She has her assets divided between TFA and T. Rowe Price. As a favor, she wanted me to call the company to sort out some IRA-related questions about beneficiaries and distributions, but it was immensely frustrating to get stuck going in circles with phone prompts, only to finally get someone on the phone who frankly had no idea what they were doing and gave us information that was incorrect. It was a forty-five-minute call that ultimately didn't even resolve the issue—maddening for both us and our client. That kind of thing is unlikely to occur when you work with a smaller local firm.

Another great example is what happened during the COVID-19 pandemic. As soon as revenues start cratering at the big-box wealth management firms, the first thing they did was cut their staff and send their loyal employees to the unemployment line. I told my employees and clients that I had absolutely no intention of having layoffs at TFA. It's during difficult times when we need our team at full strength. We have a financial plan too, and we don't panic when unforeseen events and economic downturns occur. I ask all my clients to avoid selling good investments at inopportune times, and I have made that same commitment to my people at TFA. I made this commitment while also not applying or accepting any taxpayer money in the form of a Paycheck Protection Program (PPP) loan under the CARES Act. As I mentioned earlier, I believe in a meritocracy, and this should come with a moral compass.

You can't really be a good advisor without establishing that human connection. It's really as much a people business as a money business. And I strongly believe being local, being *rooted*, having a stake in the place where you ply your trade is essential to developing that personal connection with your clientele. We're not some distant, faceless company cloistered in a glass-and-steel corporate tower; we're a local brick-and-mortar establishment with a neighborhood feel.

Look at Merrill Lynch, in contrast. It has an office here in Greensboro, as well as one in Winston-Salem and another in High Point—three branches within twenty miles of here. But Merrill is based out of New York. Is Merrill Lynch *really* interested in Greensboro? Probably not. It might have local branches here and there, but fundamentally, it's a national company, and that's where its focus lies, at the national level.

The push and pull between the big players and the smaller, independent companies is playing out in many sectors of the US economy. I wonder what the future will bring in the financial services industry, in which smaller local firms are being steadily gobbled up by bigger companies, in a wave of consolidation driven by low interest rates (making it easy for investors to borrow cash for acquisition) and the fact that a lot of veteran advisors are selling their practices as they age into retirement.

Leading the acquisitions charge are not just large wealth management companies but also private equity firms, which have no real interest in the business of financial advice; they're just (as private equity firms are wont to do) looking for cash cows. Their chop-shop approach to acquisition means they buy out smaller, successful companies, aggressively trim overhead to expand margins (which usually involves eliminating customer-friendly conveniences like a receptionist who answers the phone), all while charging the same fees as before. This kind of consolidation is beneficial to investors but generally unfavorable to consumers, especially consumers who value personal service.

I get a call probably every other week from another wealth management firm or some private equity vultures offering to buy me out. The premiums they're pitching are enticing, but my assistant knows to put those calls straight through to voice mail. I'm not interested in selling out, in letting everything we've built at TFA get absorbed into a larger entity that frankly doesn't care about Greensboro or its people.

And I really don't think they can run the business better than I can, in terms of what's in the best interest for our clients. I know they see that we're working with a loyal base of seven hundred families, and they salivate over the prospect of coming in and changing TFA from a fee-only firm to a fee-based company so they could start aggressively cross-selling: annuities, checking accounts, mortgages, lines of credit, all kinds of things. But in that case, the customer loses out.

Even if we do eventually grow into a firm with a regional or national scope (and I do want us to grow), I intend to preserve our local ethos. What's the point of expanding if you lose the very thing that made you great in the first place?

FEE-ONLY VERSUS FEE-BASED ADVISORS

People's eyes tend to glaze over whenever this topic comes up, but it's useful to understand the distinction between the two. *Fee only* describes a compensation arrangement in which advisors don't take commissions and are instead paid directly by clients on a flat fee basis or as a percentage of assets under management. This helps minimize the conflict of interest that arises when, say, they receive a bonus for selling annuities or other services; the advisor is not incentivized to push products the client doesn't really need. Fee-only advisors are true fiduciaries in that they are obligated to act in the client's best interest, even when it goes against their own.

Fee based is a somewhat misleading term (and probably deliberately so—I suspect it was cooked up by Wall Street as another slick marketing ploy). Fee-based advisors are paid via commissions in addition to compensation from the client. Fee-based advisors can't really claim to be fiduciaries, for that reason, and there's a heightened risk of conflict of interest. These advisors are licensed as registered representatives of their respective firm, meaning they represent their firm, not you.

Now there might be some very talented, dedicated, scrupulous fee-based advisors out there. But I'd strongly suggest working with fee-only firms.

You shouldn't feel like your advisor is a salesperson. Are they trying to push financial products on you each time you speak? That, too, is a red flag. These people will bleed you to death with fees and commissions.

> You shouldn't feel like your advisor is a salesperson. Are they trying to push financial products on you each time you speak? That, too, is a red flag.

You shouldn't feel like your advisor is a salesperson. Are they trying to push financial products on you each time you speak? That, too, is a red flag. These people will bleed you to death with fees and commissions.

Worse, I know multiple advisors who have sold up-front commission products like annuities, closed-end funds, unit investment trusts, or nontraded REITs, and then charged annual management fees on top of this! For example, a broker might sell an annuity and receive a 6 percent commission up front and then turn around and charge a 1 percent ongoing management fee to oversee it. The same is done with nontraded REITs. The broker takes a big commission up front and then puts that security in an advisory account where they are collecting a 1 percent annual fee. Why? These nontraded REITS are illiquid; they are "nontraded." What kind of advice and oversight is the broker providing for that fee?

Other advisors charge tremendous commissions to execute stock and bond trades, in an era when many of the big brokers (Schwab, Fidelity, TD Ameritrade) have waived trading fees for their retail customers. It's nuts.

Beware of such tricks, which serve only to siphon money from your pocket to theirs, and beware of advisors who employ them.

BALANCE OF FACE-TO-FACE SERVICE WITH TECHNOLOGY-DRIVEN CONVENIENCE

As the twenty-first century speeds along, businesses that serve the consumer market will continue to be shaped by the battle between high touch and high tech: human-driven customer service with a face or digital-driven service with a chat bot. You already know that I'm partial to a more high-touch approach, which is better suited to the nature of the financial services industry, but some consumers do favor a more digital, self-service, remotely accessible model. The younger generations, for example, are more comfortable doing everything online or over the phone, while baby boomers want to come down to the office, look you in the eye, and see you in a suit and tie in a professional office setting.

Even before the COVID-19 pandemic, we have been trying to accommodate both types of consumers with technology that allows greater at-home money management alongside the analog approach.

I do think that the rosy years of the epic bull market that started in 2009 have artificially reduced clients' interest in face-to-face meetings. When people are watching their portfolios achieve massive gains year after year, they don't have much reason to schedule meetings with their advisors. But when disaster strikes and the market trend reverses, that's when everyone wants some face time with me. It will be interesting to see if the more tech-savvy younger clients maintain their predilection for self-service, at-home, and digital advising when the bulls scatter and the bears come lumbering back into town. COVID-19 may have made that impossible for health and safety reasons for the time being, but I don't think face-to-face contact and a good old-fashioned handshake are going to be a thing of the past.

SMALL GIANTS

Bigger is not necessarily better, but there's also such a thing as too small. I'd suggest working with advising firms that hit the sweet spot between big-box behemoths and "lifestyle firms" that are basically sole proprietorships.

The ideal type firm is the "small giant" that has ten to fifty employees, offering clients the best of both worlds.

A lot of wealth management firms are just one- or two-person shops. Anybody can plant their flag, call themselves a financial advisor, and start bringing in clients. I myself was a sole practitioner for about a dozen years. But now I realize the power of working in teams and having other professionals to bounce ideas off of and help each other stay on top of our game. It's always beneficial to me to have the option to go talk to somebody else in my office and to work on a problem together. That translates into better service for our clients.

That is something that I kind of underestimated when I was younger, but when I acquired TFA, which already had twenty people under one roof, it introduced me to a new way of working. Now, I had a whole platoon of talented specialists to support me, not only with the basic stuff, like paperwork and administrative tasks, but with more substantive things, like client problems and strategic conundrums.

Recently, I changed CPAs for much this same reason. My former CPA was a great guy and very intelligent. But he was operating his own shop; it was just him and an executive assistant. While I was doing a routine check over my tax return, I noticed an oversight on his part that resulted in a tax overpayment of $48,000, a staggering amount of money to gift to the IRS. My CPA was quick to acknowledge the error, we amended the return, and the IRS adjusted my tax bill accordingly. Problem solved.

But I knew then that it was time to find a new accountant, not necessarily because of the error (we all make mistakes) but because if he had been working in an environment where there were other professionals to keep him accountable, the $48,000 mistake would never have come to pass.

So it goes with financial advisors: find a small giant type of firm where the advisors' work is subject to checks and balances by others, a place where the totality of your assets are not vested in one fallible individual, however smart they may be. Be wary of the sole practitioner who believes they can handle all of the intricacies of your financial plan and investments without more support and infrastructure. I find it fascinating to see websites of firms constantly using plural pronouns to describe a one-person firm!

TOO AGGRESSIVE OR TOO CONSERVATIVE

Successful wealth building depends on balancing risk and reward over the long term, a tricky art that is best left to the professionals. But if your advisor is either too aggressive or too conservative, it's a sign that their judgment may be lacking and your portfolio is at risk.

One of my newer clients came to me as a referral. She had been with a well-known company with $100 billion under management, a company that is known for its aggressive investment philosophy based around individual stock picking. This firm does well, so there is some merit to its high-risk approach, but it's not for everyone, and it certainly wasn't a good fit for my seventy-eight-year-old client, whose portfolio was 85 percent in forty different stocks.

We had lunch to discuss the prospect of her coming over to TFA, but during the meal, she was always on her phone checking to see if her portfolio was up or down for the day—constantly looking at the ticker as her French onion soup went cold.

"Ma'am, you're seventy-eight years old," I said. "Is this really how you want to spend your retirement, with your eyes glued to the daily ups and downs of the market? Even I don't do that."

No, she admitted, it wasn't.

And it's all fun and games in a roaring bull market where each day closes in the green, but what about during the next downturn? I asked her what kind of loss she'd be comfortable sustaining at her age, and she said 10 percent. But I cautioned her that with such a risky portfolio allocation, she could sustain a 10 percent dip in her net worth in a matter of days.

She already had enough income from Social Security and her pension. She didn't need the potential double-digit returns from a portfolio lopsided toward equities. Her advisor never should have allowed it. It was downright reckless. And it was time for her to make a change. She ended up signing up with TFA, which rebalanced her assets to a more conservative allocation, and I'm confident she enjoys greater peace of mind as a result. In fact, during the downturn in the first quarter of 2020, she thanked me profusely for reallocating her into a more appropriate portfolio.

Then on the flip side, some advisors are overly cautious and fall prey to the doom-and-gloom drumbeat of those people who are always yelling, "Sell, sell, sell! The end is nigh!" If you are too conservative, with high allocations in cash and bonds, you may not be able to achieve all the goals you've identified in your financial plan. Beware the advisor who pushes you into a chronically conservative approach (preretirement or early in retirement).

COVER ALL THE BASES

Anyone who's played or watched baseball knows the pitcher doesn't just stand inert when the ball is in play, even if it's nowhere near the pitcher. If the ball is hit into the outfield, the pitcher needs to be ready to cut off an errant throw from the outfielder. He might need to back up a throw to second or third if it sails past his teammate. If a base runner is charging home while the catcher is fielding the ball, the pitcher must cover home plate. Pitching demands a lot more than, well, pitching.

It's the same with financial advising. I think there are a lot of poor advisors who just don't do much in the way of financial planning. They focus entirely on the investments, but you can't implement a disciplined and prudent investment strategy without a comprehensive financial plan to provide a foundation for the client's financial goals. Many advisors also fail to consistently review their clients' tax returns, legal documents, education savings plans, Social Security, Medicare, 401(k)s, insurance, and so on.

That's not acceptable. All of these intertwining components make up a person's financial life, so a good advisor considers everything at once. Pick one who keeps their eye on the ball.

TAKEAWAYS:

1. The CFP certification is the gold standard in the industry, and unlike a lot of titles appended to an advisor's name, it carries weight. Having a CFP is a strong indication the person is a cut above his or her peers.

2. Choosing the right advisor comes down to trust: are you confident they'll manage your money well and dispense the right advice at the right time? Do you feel comfortable sharing private details about your personal and family life? How would you describe your relationship with them: fiduciary-client or salesperson-prospect?

3. All things considered, the best firms out there are often the small giants that offer a Goldilocks medium between gargantuan national wire houses and one-person shops.

CONCLUSION

BUILDING WEALTH WITH CONFIDENCE

The United States has always been a mobile nation: most of us end up settling far afield from where we grew up, lured by relationships, professional opportunities, or just the same spirit of adventure that has always animated the American people.

I left home twice before I found my place in the world, here in Greensboro. The first time was kind of a false start—I spent my freshman year of college at the University of Alabama on a baseball scholarship, but it wasn't a good fit, and by the following fall I had transferred to IIT, a few miles from my hometown.

IIT was better for me, and most importantly, I still had a spot on the starting roster. Playing pro baseball was my plan for the future; sports was the only thing I really knew or could imagine doing. I understood the odds of making it to the majors were infinitesimally small, but good pitchers are always in demand, and I had a blistering fastball that blew batters away.

However, my athletic skills did not blossom as easily as I had hoped. In what was probably my first lesson about the value of diversification, coaches told me I had to expand my repertoire of pitches. My heater did not intimidate college sluggers the way it had left high schoolers swinging at empty air, and I struggled to add off-speed stuff and breaking balls (curves, sliders) and develop the control pitchers need to paint the inside, throw outside, go high and low, and so on.

> The dissolution of my dreams on the diamond paved the way for a plan B career as a financial advisor and entrepreneur, and I'm confident my plan B has worked out better for me than my plan A would have.

Athletic success had come effortlessly in high school, but when it became apparent that advancing my baseball career would require me to work and grind and sacrifice, I lost my passion for the game (a bum elbow didn't help either), and with it, my life plan.

As so often happens in life, what initially seems a great setback proves to be a blessing in disguise. The dissolution of my dreams on the diamond paved the way for a plan B career as a financial advisor and entrepreneur, and I'm confident my plan B has worked out better for me than my plan A would have.

But that career didn't materialize overnight, and I spent the next several years after college caught between past and future, youth and adulthood, inertia and clarity of purpose.

For a few years, I worked on the floor of the Chicago Mercantile Exchange, then later for a small financial planning firm. During this time I completed my MBA and earned my CFP. But this was a bad time to be a financial advisor; the markets were anemic after the dot-com bubble and 9/11, and it was painful to see clients' account values drop year after year from 2000 to 2002. It weighed on me—I felt like I was letting people down. And though I was content with my job, I also felt like my position wasn't allowing me to realize my full potential.

By that point, I was in my midtwenties, and except for that brief foray in Alabama, I had never lived anywhere but the Chicago area. Family, friends, and familiarity kept me tethered to my hometown. All in all, it was a good life. But would I really spend the rest of it there?

My friends were a fantastic group of guys who were extremely loyal, and from the age of twelve, we were inseparable. We would have lain down in traffic for each other. We're still very close. But many of them would readily admit that I had a chance to achieve more than they did in life, and I needed to jump on opportunities, even if that meant leaving everything behind. That opportunity came in the form of an interview with First Horizon, a mortgage company that was looking to expand into wealth management and was hiring a CFP in Greensboro.

One of my best friends was Fish, a guy I'd known since we were nine-year-olds playing Little League together. Dan's his real name, but I never heard anyone but his mom call him that. To us, he was always Fish.

Fish was a man of few words, but a conversation we had one evening has stuck with me. It was unusual for any of us guys to engage with serious topics; our conversations were usually based on the amicable exchange of good-natured insults and jabs. But that night, Fish and I were ruminating on the future. I mentioned the upcoming interview and that I was considering leaving Chicago. I didn't know how he would react, but Fish said I needed to go after it instead of hanging around the same people I grew up with and doing the same things we had done since high school.

It was an eye-opening moment. I knew he was right.

In Greensboro, I was interviewed by Kelly Starkey, who remains a good friend to this day. Within a week I said my goodbyes to everyone in Chicago and moved into a temporary apartment in Greensboro. It was a major change and a big challenge, but I felt ready. An ironic outcome of my short-circuited baseball career was that it inspired a powerful determination to excel in whatever pursuit I undertook—to never again taste the bitter pill of failure. That determination has been a unifying thread through my whole career and still motivates me today.

Today, in my position at the helm of TFA, I don't want to let anyone down: my clients, my employees, my family, my parents, myself. That's why I'm constantly trying to improve in this business, trying to find better ways to help clients plan for the future and save, invest, and distribute money.

I'm grateful to get up each morning and go to work knowing that what we're doing makes a real difference—in the lives of our hundreds of clients and their families and for the thousands of people who have taken the Retirement 101 seminar I've taught for seventeen years. I'm grateful for the daily challenges and problem solving that make my occupation interesting, for the people I work with, and for the students and the clients and the people of Greensboro who support us and trust us.

I can't speak for the rest of the industry, with its headlong, head-strong charge toward consolidation and digitization, but at TFA, we'll never lose the independence and the human touch that have earned us accolades from *Barron's*, *Forbes*, and the *Financial Times* and made us into one of the premier firms in the country.

At the end of the day, it's the human side of the business that matters most. What good is a robo-advisor or a "Please hold, your call is very important to us" 1-800 number for someone who has just become permanently disabled at a young age or for someone whose spouse was just diagnosed with dementia? What do you

> At the end of the day, it's the human side of the business that matters most.

do if a personal crisis forces you to shift from plan A to plan B in a heartbeat? In such moments, you're going to want to work with someone whose door you can knock on, whose hand you can shake, and whose face you know, and not just because you've met him in his office but because you see him out shopping for groceries or playing at the playground with his kids.

I think of some of our clients and the struggles they've been through, like the young doctor whose epilepsy will prevent him from ever working again. When faced with something like that, you're not even on plan B anymore. You're working on plan C, plan D—a long-term challenge that forces you to adapt and stay on your toes just to stay one step ahead of the problem.

You experience this kind of thing a lot in this business. Two of my clients are a couple in their fifties. Everything was going well for them, and they were fully on track with their financial plan, until their college-age son got caught up in drugs and overdosed. Now he's battling a serious addiction. His parents are with him in that battle, but all their lives are changed now, perhaps permanently. In a flash they went from having everything under control to facing one of the toughest crises a parent ever has to face. Moments like that force you to figure out what your priorities are.

As an advisor, that's what moves me—the ability to help people in their worst moments as well as their best. That's what really counts.

And the more I experience in my own life, the better I can serve our clients. Between raising children, being married for a significant period of time, and now dealing with aging parents whose health is in decline, there's a lot about being a good advisor that you can't learn in a book. There's no certification test for empathy. It takes having to go through some of those experiences yourself or sharing in those experiences with your clients.

LIVING LIFE WITH INTENTION

Life, by nature, is uncertain and ever changing. But living with intention doesn't mean having all the answers all the time. On the contrary, part of it is simply moving with the ebb and flow of life, secure in your vision at the core while acknowledging the fluidity and unpredictability at the margins.

No one taught me that better than David O'Neal, a guy who started as a consultant with TFA before eventually rising to chief operating officer (COO)—and, most importantly, a good friend. David was all about living with intention; it was his gospel, which he spread with the fervor and charisma of a Sunday preacher. He boiled it down to three essential questions: "What's the life you want to live?

Do you have the resources to live that life? And ultimately, are you prepared for life's surprises?"

I ask these questions of clients, but I also ask them of myself, to check myself and make sure I'm on the right path. They're useful for anyone to gain focus and do a little introspection.

David impressed us so much as a consultant that we eventually hired him as our COO. He certainly had the managerial chops for the position, but what really won me over was his infectious energy. With his George Clooney-like good looks and effortless charm, any room he walked into, he was going to own it.

His relentless optimism was a refreshing jolt for the whole organization, and his very presence encouraged people around him, including me, to step up their game. He was also the one who, along with another TFA advisor, came up with the company motto of "live with intention."

At the time, I hadn't even heard the phrase, but we ran with it because it resonated with what we were trying to do as financial planners and wealth managers—not merely make money but make money with purpose, to give people the clarity to figure out what they really want out of life and help them charge forward to get it.

When he came on board, David was actually living in Seattle and would commute to North Carolina, two weeks on, two weeks off. Once his kids had gone off to college, he and his wife, Jane, planned to move full time to Greensboro.

One day, David and Jane were playing tennis with Christina and me. In between sets, as David ran to grab some water, Jane confided that she had had to rush him to the ER the previous night because of some respiratory problems. From the way he was zipping around the court and smashing our serves back over the net, you'd never know it. That's the kind of energy he had.

And yet, shortly thereafter, our worst fears were proven true: David was diagnosed with nonsmoker's lung cancer. It had already spread to his bones and brain.

He took time off work to convalesce back on the West Coast, but we talked regularly. "Don't worry, Patrick; I'm gonna kick cancer's ass," he would tell me. And I believed it. But then I started getting messages from him that seemed, well, off. "I love you, man." Sentimental stuff like that, just a little uncharacteristic. Was the medication making him a little loopy, or was he trying to say goodbye?

Not long after that, Jane texted me with a devastating announcement: "It's taken a turn for the worse. He's in hospice now at home."

"What the hell happened?" I thought. I knew the prognosis had been grim, but I thought if anyone could beat it, it'd be David.

His fifty-third birthday was coming up, so I thought I'd fly out to Seattle and surprise him.

"That sounds great, but I have to tell you, I can't promise he will be here," Jane said.

Sure enough, a few days later, on a rainy Monday morning (the day before my flight and his birthday), I received another text from her: "David passed away overnight." I still just couldn't believe it. Even now, it's hard to process how a man with such exuberant energy, such a bright inner light, was taken so young and in such a short period of time.

If there's any consolation, it's that David managed to touch so many people during his life. His infectious positivity continues to reverberate here at TFA, where "live with intention" remains our guiding philosophy. In this way, he's indirectly influenced hundreds if not thousands of clients we've worked with. He's certainly inspired me and made me approach my own life and work with the same spirit.

Living with intention means executing plans with diligence and clarity but accepting the randomness of the universe. We can't control the unknown, but we can be sure never to take anything for granted.

For me, a big part of intentionality is also refusing to settle for mediocrity. That's probably one of the reasons David and I got along so well—we recognized in each other the drive to always do better. And if your job is managing other people's money, you can't settle for second rate.

As for my own approach to living with intention, at forty-four years old, I'm still undecided about some things. Sometimes you go down one path that you think is perfect for you, only to

> Living with intention means executing plans with diligence and clarity but accepting the randomness of the universe. We can't control the unknown, but we can be sure never to take anything for granted.

realize that it wasn't as meaningful as you expected. Or something that you thought was important doesn't bring as much satisfaction as you had hoped. The usual existential doubts that just take time, experience, and trial and error to figure out.

Despite working long hours and enduring the stress of running a business, I feel blessed—for my beautiful loving wife and three healthy kids, the love and support of parents and siblings, the ability to positively affect my clients' lives, career success along with accolades and respect in the industry, playing an influential role in the community, and of course, good health. What more could an ex-baseball player from Chicago ask for?

I'm immensely grateful that I'm able to live my ideal life. I hope the lessons in this book help you live yours too.

ACKNOWLEDGMENTS

To the founder of TFA, Carter Leinster, for being a mentor and a friend. You took a chance on me in 2011 and gave me the opportunity of a lifetime. You were a pioneer for women in the wealth management industry, and your confidence and passion have inspired many throughout the years. I am eternally grateful, Carter.

To Paul Megliola, for introducing me to the aforementioned Carter Leinster. You have been instrumental in my career growth and continue to be an excellent consultant, advocate, and friend.

I want to thank Don DeRosa for challenging me as a professional from the day we met. You trusted me to manage your lifelong savings after interviewing many financial advisors, and I can always count on you to hold me accountable.

I want to thank the late David O'Neal for being a friend and an inspiration. Your energy was infectious, and you challenged me to think big and bold. I miss you dearly.

To all the clients I have had the pleasure to work with and the team at TFA I have been honored to work alongside—past and present. I believe our industry should be a meritocracy, and you inspire me to constantly get better and raise the bar.

To the team at Advantage|ForbesBooks, including David Ferris, Josh Houston, Rachel Griffin, and Alison Morse: for keeping me on task, giving me words of encouragement, and helping me create an excellent book.

And finally, I want to thank my wife, Christina, and our children. Christina, for your love, patience, and listening skills, as well as your extraordinary ability to always keep me focused on doing what's right instead of what's easy. And to our children (Havana, Walker, and Quincy), who bring me the greatest joy and make life seem so simple, yet inspire me to accomplish so much more. I hope you read this book and understand that money means more than dinosaurs, Legos, and Roblox.

ABOUT THE AUTHOR

Patrick Rush has been providing financial planning and investment advice since 1998. He is the CEO of Triad Financial Advisors in Greensboro, North Carolina, and is a practicing Certified Financial Planner™ professional. He has consistently received national recognition as a top financial advisor by *Forbes*, *Barron's*, and the *Financial Times*, and his firm was awarded by the Invest in Others Charitable Foundation as a "Charitable Champion." Patrick was previously the president of independent wealth management and also served individuals and families as a vice president and senior financial advisor at Merrill Lynch.

Patrick earned his BS in financial markets and trading from the Illinois Institute of Technology as well as an MBA in finance from the Stuart School of Business. He is the author and instructor of Retirement 101, a course designed to teach the fundamentals of financial planning and investment management to both preretirees and retirees. Patrick is a fierce advocate of the view that all financial advisors should be held to the fiduciary standard. In addition, he believes implementing a low-cost evidenced-based investment philosophy alongside a comprehensive financial plan will provide his clients the greatest likelihood for a successful outcome.

Patrick resides in Greensboro with his wife, Dr. Christina Rush, their daughter, Havana, and their twin boys, Walker and Quincy.

OUR SERVICES

Triad Financial Advisors (TFA) is an independent, fee-only SEC-registered registered investment advisor (RIA) with a mission to help clients live, invest, and retire with intention. Recognized as one of the top wealth management firms in the country by *Forbes*, *Barron's*, and the *Financial Times*, TFA is unique because we require all our advisors to have earned the CFP® certification. Thus, our clients can find comfort in knowing our diverse team of advisors has the knowledge, experience, and ethics to build a comprehensive financial plan. In addition, TFA uses a customized, low-cost, evidence-based investment philosophy to give clients the highest probability of a successful long-term investment experience.

The foundation of our service model begins with the financial plan and identifying the goals of our clients. In simple terms, we help determine the following:

1. What is the life you want to live?

2. Do you have the resources to make that achievable?

3. Are you prepared for the curveballs that life can throw your way?

We can then build a financial plan that encompasses the following:

- Cash flow and retirement income needs

- Net worth statement

- Liquidity

- Debt management

- Asset management and investment philosophy

- Tax planning

- Insurance needs

- Estate planning

- Charitable giving

More information about Triad Financial Advisors can be located at www.triadfa.com.